THE
BROTHERHOOD
OF THE
DISAPPEARING
PANTS

Also by the Authors:

Sweet Jesus, I Hate Bill O'Reilly

Fair and Balanced, My Ass! An Unbridled Look at the Bizarre Reality of Fox News

THE
BROTHERHOOD
OF THE
DISAPPEARING
PANTS

A Field Guide to
CONSERVATIVE SEX SCANDALS

Joseph Minton Amann
and Tom Breuer
Preface by Larry Flynt

NATION
BOOKS

www.nationbooks.org

THE BROTHERHOOD OF THE DISAPPEARING PANTS:
A Field Guide to Conservative Sex Scandals

Copyright © 2007 Joseph Minton Amann and Tom Breuer
Preface copyright © 2007 Larry Flynt

Published by
Nation Books
A Member of the Perseus Books Group
116 East 16th Street, 8th Floor
New York, NY 10003

Nation Books is a copublishing venture of the Nation Institute
and the Perseus Books Group.

Nation Books titles are available at special discounts for bulk purchases in the United
States by corporations, institutions, and other organizations. For more information,
please contact the Special Markets Department at the Perseus Books Group,
2300 Chestnut Street, Suite 200, Philadelphia, PA 19103, or call (800) 255-1514,
or e-mail special.markets@perseusbooks.com.

Library of Congress Cataloging-in-Publication Data is available.

ISBN-10: 1-56858-377-X
ISBN-13: 978-1-56858-377-8

9 8 7 6 5 4 3 2 1

Book design by Astrid E. deRidder

Printed in the United States of America

CONTENTS

Section II | *Religiousia Devianti* 131

Section III | *Conservativicus Debaucheria* 177

PREFACE

Hats off to Joseph Minton Amann and Tom Breuer! By putting together this easy-to-use field guide they have made it much easier to keep track of Republican sexual hypocrisy. Up until now, it's been an awesome task; there are just too many Republican sex scandals to keep track of—even for me and my knowledgeable, dedicated staff. On top of that, the list of Republican hypocrites gets bigger, seemingly by the day.

It is with particular pride that I note the names of Rep. Bob Livingston and Rep. Bob Barr in this book. While I have put the spotlight on numerous Republican hypocrites in an effort to expose them for what they are, those two are my own personal trophies, brought down by information I obtained when I ran an ad in the Washington Post back in 1998.

In any case, you are about to take a tour into the right wing's political underbelly, courtesy of Amann and Breuer. Within these pages you will discover the ugly truth about who your political and religious leaders really are, not just in terms of their sex drives but also in terms of their respect for truth and honesty.

A careful reading of this book should convince you that there are more sexual hijinks taking place in Washington, D.C., than you'll ever find in the pages of Hustler.

Larry Flynt

INTRODUCTION

"You could write about liberal scandals, too."
—Tom's mom

"Well, at least it doesn't have 'Jesus' in the title."
—Joe's mom

When we hit upon the idea of a book on political sex scandals, it was clear from the start which direction we would go with it.

Not only had we already established something of a reputation as the Gore Vidal and Howard Zinn of the 300-page, wide-margined book with lots of profanity and *Match Game* references (see *Sweet Jesus, I Hate Bill O'Reilly,* and *Fair and Balanced, My Ass! An Unbridled Look at the Bizarre Reality of Fox News*), it was also evident that sowing our seed among the rocky, humorless soil of Democratic peccadilloes was pretty pointless when there was so much rich Republican loam to be had.

So while Tom labored through the Feast of St. Peter, all of Lent, and two-thirds of Easter Sunday liturgy before letting his mother in on the joke, and Joe never did have the heart to tell *his* mom that the working title was *Jesus Gets It On with Mary Magdalene and Other Conservative Sex Scandals,* there never really was any doubt where all this was eventually going to lead.

But, you might fairly ask, why limit the book's scope? Doesn't a reference guide on exclusively conservative scandals run the risk of feeling sort of stifled and truncated? Certainly both sides live in glass houses, and we do so enjoy throwing stones.

Well, quite honestly, a sex scandal is a little like a work of art. It's hard to describe what works, but you know it when you see it. And quite frankly, when it comes to the art of the sex scandal, conservatives are Botticellis and Kandinskys while liberals are left sitting in the corner, biting their lips in deep thought as they struggle to draw the profile of the pirate for their application to correspondence school.

You see, the magic ingredients that make Republicans such artful dodgers and Democrats so dull by comparison are abundant hypocrisy and insufferable sanctimony.

Boning your secretary is certainly bad form, but it's hardly worth mentioning anymore unless you happen to be a family values conservative or chairman emeritus of the local Anti-Boning-Your-Secretary League. These days, you need plenty of irony to keep that particular beach ball in the air.

Of course, it also depends on who you are and how broad your sexual tastes run. If you're Madeleine Albright and you're getting it from K-Fed, it's gonna make the news.

But a Democratic governor getting busted for having an affair with some guy on his payroll, then proudly announcing, "I'm a gay American" before booking himself a guest slot on *Oprah?* Kind of a snooze.

A self-righteous jackass of an evangelical preacher begging for your forgiveness after buying male prostitutes and methamphetamine with tithes he scammed from little old ladies, then showing up about two days later in a documentary on youth Bible camps making creepy joking references to gay sex? Pants-wetting hilarious.

Of course, we also feel this book has a certain utilitarian value. You know that annoying relative who still tells that same lame joke about Bill and Monica every Thanksgiving right around the time the pie gets passed around? Consider this a rebuttal.

So as we venture through these verdant fields, remember that, while there is surely room for a book on liberal sex scandals, it's just as surely a project for someone else—maybe Ken Starr or one of Sean Hannity's research assistants.

What you *will* see are conservatives of every stripe—some you know, others whom you'll grow to know and love. And it will soon become as clear as the falafel in front of you that conserva-tives hardly have a monopoly on morality and family values.

In fact, when you get them behind closed doors they can be downright freaky.

No, seriously. *Really* freaky.

So sit back, relax, and try not to get the vapors. It's gonna be a heckuva ride.

Section I
Republicanicus Libidinus

For years now the GOP has tried to corner the market on family values, regularly warning of the dread influence of liberalism in America. Whether it be the dangers of "San Francisco values" or those God-hating Hollywood elites, the political right has done a brilliant job of painting themselves as the voice of traditionalism in America. Yet a little research shows how it's not all post-nuptial missionary-position boot knocking for the far right. What you'll often find instead is deviant sexuality repressed to the breaking point. And when they do finally break, these upstanding leaders of community and country make an East Village leather bar look like a Hello Kitty–themed bat mitzvah.

The first section of this compendium examines the conservative politician and his bizarre and complex mating habits. From Mark Foley to Neil Bush to the bounders behind the Clinton impeachment, you'll see there's more kinky stuff happening on the right side of the aisle than in all the swinger bars from the Castro District to Key West.

1.

The Sex Club–Loving Land-of-Lincoln Trekker

Common Name:
Jack Ryan

Native Habitat:
Parisian sex clubs

Distincive Behavior:
Pursues public
copulation

The butterfly effect—the notion, made famous by the film of the same name, that small changes in a particular set of circumstances can lead to oversized effects later—has led to plenty of late-night counterfactual historical musings over the fates of mankind, in addition to inspiring more than its share of turgid sci-fi potboilers.

So it's especially fitting that a man's request of his wife that she do the nasty in a public place might someday lead directly to Barack Obama, who just a few short years ago was a little-known state senator from Illinois, becoming the next president of the United States.

But that's getting ahead of the story a little.

In the beginning, Jeri Ryan was just another TV star. After making numerous TV guest appearances and appearing in a few unremarkable films, she landed her big break as the inimitably pneumatic Seven of Nine on *Star Trek: Voyager*.

But though she was by no means Jennifer Aniston, her popularity grew—and with it the inherent joys and perils of being a *Star Trek* celebrity.

And while knowing with metaphysical certainty that somewhere in the world a single, middle-aged man's little admiral—made preternaturally rigid by your latest photo spread in *Sci Fi Magazine*—is being chafed beyond recognition by nacho cheese residue and a Diamond Select Star Trek 40th Anniversary Phaser–callused hand is no doubt creepy beyond words, it's a small price to pay for enduring fame.

And so it was that, in the midst of the prosperous late '90s, when so many Americans were looking at the future with rose-colored glasses, Jeri Ryan's life looked pretty close to perfect.

She was married to Jack Ryan, a wealthy investment banker, and the couple had a healthy son. And though her marriage would later end in divorce, she continued to get work, while Jack became a rising star in Illinois Republican circles.

But Jack's beliefs had unfortunately opened him up to unusual scrutiny. Indeed, his Christian conservative views clearly informed his politics. Not only did he oppose same-sex marriage, but civil unions and registries as well. He believed in the most traditional definition of marriage and, at least on the surface, appeared to practice what he preached.

Indeed, Jack was the kind of husband women dreamed about. Handsome and romantic, he loved springing surprise trips on his wife from time to time and in 1998 took her on three unplanned sojourns to New Orleans, New York, and Paris. But Jack's veneer of respectability was as thin as the Mylar wrapping on a George Takei–autographed *Star Trek V* novelization.

You see, on their "surprise trips," Jack began telling his wife that he wanted to go where no future Illinois Senate candidate had gone before—to exotic Terran sex clubs with his famous TV wife. She refused at first, but eventually gave in.

Shortly thereafter, the couple would divorce, and the gory details were to be sealed forever. At least that was God's plan, before the liberal media decided to stick its nose in.

As Ryan defeated seven primary opponents to secure the GOP nomination, he insisted that his divorce records stay sealed to protect his son. Jack even went so far as to assure Judy Baar Topinka, the Republican state chairwoman, that the sealed divorce records contained nothing that would embarrass the campaign.

Oh, but the press is a harsher mistress than most—or at least most that you'd find anywhere outside of an avant-garde Paris sex club. Eventually, the *Chicago Tribune* and a local television station filed suit to have the couple's divorce and custody records unsealed. A Los Angeles Superior Court allowed it, while also allowing some passages to be redacted.

It turned out the records were a touch embarrassing after all. Jeri detailed some of her marriage's greatest hits, including Jack's sex-club fetish. She talked about a "bizarre club" they visited in New York with "cages, whips, and other apparatus hanging from the ceiling."

"Respondent wanted me to have sex with him there, with another couple watching. I refused. Respondent asked me to perform a sexual activity upon him, and he specifically asked other people to watch. I was very upset. We left the club and respondent apologized, said that I was right and he would never insist that I go to a club again. He promised it was out of his system."

Now, while promising your beautiful and accomplished wife that you'll never make her go to a club where people engage in public sex acts again is hardly a Hallmark moment, it did show a modicum of sensitivity. It's not candles, rose petals, and breakfast in bed, but it's not a spiked leather bra, gimp mask, and a double-ended dildo either. One might say it nicely splits the difference.

Oh, but if only men could actually keep their promises that they wouldn't have to make in the first place if they weren't selfish, sexually depraved skeevs.

Apparently, it *wasn't* out of his system. They still had Paris.

In court documents, Jeri told of the couple's fairytale journey to the most romantic city in the world, and their little side trip to a sex club: "People were having sex everywhere. I cried. I was physically ill." Her compassionate conservative husband then allegedly told her it wasn't a "turn on" for her to cry.

Jack's version was slightly different. He recalled the trips as "romantic getaways," saying "we did go to one avant-garde nightclub in Paris, which was more than either one of us felt comfortable with. We left and vowed never to return."

How gallant.

But even after the cork was off the Hai Karate bottle, Ryan firmly believed he was still in the race:

"I think that when voters look into their hearts and minds and say, 'Can we trust this fellow Jack Ryan, or does he try to do the best he can, or is he in this job for the right reasons?' I think they'll see that same sincerity to try to do the right thing, though knowing that in the end that I am human and I do fail."

No, degrading your wife in a Parisian sex club is not a "failing" and it's not even really human. Add to it the knowledge that your wife is a highly recognizable public figure, it takes on an even more disquieting quality. Seriously, *Star Trek* fans—many of whom would give their left dilithium crystal for a brief glimpse of Jeri Ryan's sock drawer—are everywhere. What if an incriminating video had found its way onto the Web?

But as cornered animals are apt to do, Jack got more aggressive. During a June 22, 2004, radio interview, he referred to the publicity as "a new low for politics."

Three days later, he released a statement about his troubled candidacy: "Thirteen months ago I announced my determination to seek the Republican nomination for the United States Senate. I entered the race because I love my country and my home state of Illinois and because I believe that one man, living for purposes larger than himself, can make a difference.

"The media has gotten out of control. The fact that the *Chicago Tribune* sues for access to sealed custody documents and then takes unto itself the right to publish details of a custody dispute—over the objections of two parents who agree that the reairing of their arguments will hurt their ability to co-parent their child and will hurt their child—is truly outrageous."

It went on for a while after that, but the two things that most stood out were (1) there was no mention of his affinity for hardcore sex in front of strangers; and (2) he was withdrawing from the race.

But, as was alluded to earlier, Jack's inability to become sufficiently aroused by the sight of Jeri Ryan's naked body could ultimately end up having enormous consequences.

At the time Ryan withdrew from his Senate bid, he was battling a young little-known state senator named Barack Obama. The GOP scrambled to replace Ryan and eventually settled on political retread and certified right-wing nutburger Alan Keyes.

Now, a Senate race in a moderate Midwestern state with no incumbent on the ballot would ordinarily be expected to be pretty close. The Republicans could have run Count Chocula and been confident about getting 30 percent of the vote. Instead, they ran Keyes—and got 27 percent.

The charismatic Obama sailed to victory and onto the national stage, from which he could very well be poised to make history as our nation's first African American president.

Indeed, when asked about Ryan's scandalous court documents, Obama was characteristically statesmanlike: "I don't think it's appropriate for me to comment on that. Those are issues of personal morality. The issues I'm focused on are public morality."

Happily, the authors are not nearly as gracious.

2.

The Great Floridian Instant-Messaging Teen-Page Predator

Common Name:
Mark Foley

Native Habitat:
World Wide Web

Natural Enemies:
Reporters; lose-
lipped pages

Distinctive Call:
"Grab the one-eyed
snake"

What was the most outrageous part about the Mark Foley midterm sex spectacular, which embroiled the GOP in scandal in the fall of 2006?

The creepy instant messages? The alleged cover-ups? The realization that a fraction of our tax dollars, however small, was being diverted to the subscription departments at *Tiger Beat* and *Boy Fancy?*

No, the worst part was that Foley masqueraded as an indefatigable child protector while simultaneously perving out in the hallowed halls of Congress.

Indeed, perhaps more than anything else, Republicans' fortunes were undermined in '06 by the Florida congressman's tireless efforts both to establish a national sex offender database and to keep his own name out of it.

Of course, Foley was derailed before he could either fulfill his wildest pederastic wishes or develop the world's first fully functional sodomy emoticon, but voters could hardly fail to notice that this particular fox had not only long since infiltrated the henhouse, but had eagerly begun plucking and loading up on Crisco.

As chairman of the House Caucus on Missing and Exploited Children, Foley sunk to almost unfathomable depths of hypocrisy in a town already legendary for its hypocrites. It was as if, at the height of the civil rights struggles of the 1960s, Strom Thurmond had chaired the Senate Select Committee on Not Having an Illegitimate Negro Daughter.

For instance, Foley introduced a bill that would ban "child modeling" Web sites that offered no services or products outside of simply viewing the models. "These Web sites are nothing more than a fix for pedophiles," asserted Foley.

He added, "They don't sell products, they don't sell services—all they serve are young children on a platter for America's most depraved. These sites sell child erotica and they should be banned."

Of course, if these sites really were buffets for child predators, Foley himself was likely to be the first in line asking where they keep the hot plates.

But while several wags helpfully pointed out at the time the cognitive dissonance inherent in Foley's public and private stances toward studly pages, if anything the uproar was muted somewhat by a suddenly compassionate conservative press.

For instance, shortly after the Foley page scandal first made headlines, Fox News's Bill O'Reilly came off as uncharacteristically reserved in his scorn.

On the September 29, 2006, *O'Reilly Factor,* O'Reilly introduced the Foley flap as "a very disturbing story," mentioning Foley's past advocacy on behalf of children, particularly the congressman's support of Jessica's Law, which establishes harsh minimum penalties for child predators.

Discussing the Foley case with Fox reporter Major Garrett, O'Reilly appeared almost to be drumming up sympathy for Foley: "Yes. You know, a real tragedy here, Major. I know you're just reporting and you don't comment as a reporter. But the real tragedy is that Foley did some good work, you know, getting the database up, the federal database to track child predators."

With all due respect, Mr. O'Reilly, the "real tragedy" was that a duly elected member of Congress was about a monkey and a carousel away from making the United States House of Representatives his own personal Neverland Ranch.

Then again, a visit Foley had previously made to *The O'Reilly Factor* would prove rather illuminating. In 2003, fellow culture warriors Foley and O'Reilly discussed one of the great dangers facing Western civilization: family nudist camps: "Well Bill, we're talking about kids, impressionable young kids that are being put together in camps that I think are not only degrading to them, but dangerous to their well being. People that are working around these camps, people that are peering through the fences can have significant ill intent. And so this is like putting a match next to a gas can. It's sooner or later going to explode and there'll be real dangerous consequences."

In an eerie bit of foreshadowing, Foley later added, "Kids deserve protection. People that are under the age of eighteen need supervision by someone who will look out for them."

Now, whether or not family nudist camps are a grave and gathering danger is really beyond the purview of this book. It falls into the category of "things that have no discernible impact on 99.999 percent of the population." But then the thought of going to a beach with a bunch of pasty, screaming families is nauseating enough when they're clothed. Their being naked doesn't make it suddenly erotic. If anything it's more irritating.

But in Foley's defense, he was, in his own way, doing what he could to look out for the kids. Indeed, back in 2003, the same year he warned O'Reilly about the pernicious influence of family nudist camps, he had this instant message exchange with a fully clothed teenage boy:

"how my favorite young stud doing"

We can only assume here that Foley is inquiring as to the status of the boy's horse.

"did any girl give you a hand job this weekend"

Okay, so he wasn't talking about a horse. But he was showing an interest in the young man's activities. Certainly that falls under compassionate conservatism or child protection or something in that vein.

"well I have a totally stiff wood now"

Okay, so maybe "child protection" is stretching it. In fact, when it comes to sexually aggressive behavior toward a subordinate, this is often referred to in clinical terms as "taking the exit to O'Reillyville."

"get a ruler and measure it for me"

Okay, the guy is just a creep.

But even though this stuff already made him sound like he was attending an open casting call for NBC's *To Catch a Predator,* he was far from finished.

Were this a K-tel collection of Foley's greatest hits, you'd also get "did you spank it this weekend yourself" and the international pop sensation "where do you unload it." But that's not all. At no extra cost, you'll receive the soothing soft ballad "i always use lotion and the hand" and that timeless rock classic "grab the one eyed snake."

Back in 2003, shortly after his interview with Foley aired, O'Reilly read a letter from one of his viewers: "I was recently at a nude camp. The youth were well supervised, well mannered, and comfortable with the environment. I challenge Congressman Foley to visit.'"

Well, dear viewer, you might want that tour guide to bring a tranquilizer gun.

3.
The Extraordinary In-Flight Heavy Petter

Common Name:
Galen Fox

Mating Grounds:
Soaring at
35,000 feet

Distinctive Behavior:
Uninvited
in-flight foreplay

The preflight instructions on domestic airliners can be an interminable ordeal. Indeed, most of us zone out somewhere between the part about the oxygen masks dropping down in the event of a sudden change in cabin pressure and the part about not rubbing the vagina of the person sitting next to you.

Former Hawaii legislator Galen Fox is unlikely ever to make that mistake again.

On December 18, 2004, Fox joined the exclusive mile yuck club when he fondled a stranger on a flight from Honolulu to Los Angeles.

As a spokesman for the Assistant U.S. Attorney's office in Los Angeles told the AP: "The woman testified that she was asleep, and she woke up and Mr. Fox's hand was in between her legs and the zipper of her pants was down, and that's essentially the gist of the case."

Still, as Hawaii-to-LA in-flight State House Republican hoo-hoo stroking stories go, this one is pretty weird.

It all started when a 27-year-old woman

took a late-night United Airlines flight with her parents en route to Vegas via LA. The woman in question reported that, prior to the incident, she took a Dramamine and fell asleep. According to a story in the *Honolulu Star-Bulletin,* the woman then "awoke to a warm sensation against her crotch and discovered the male passenger in the seat next to her, later identified as Fox, had his hands in her jeans and was rubbing her crotch."

The woman then promptly reported the incident to the flight attendants on duty because, you know, gross.

The *Star-Bulletin* reported that the incident had rattled the woman, leading to anxiety, fear, and numbness, as well as difficulties concentrating and sleeping.

Fox's statements, on the other hand, were more inconsistent, ranging from gut-wrenchingly revolting to bathing-in-baby-seal-blood-while-feasting-on-live-kitten-entrails-and-parboiled-toddler-hearts abhorrent.

Despite being convicted and resigning from the Legislature at the urging of Republican Governor Linda Lingle, Fox appeared to believe he had been treated unfairly.

"She said things about what I did that were just absolutely untrue. And I said, you know, what I thought had happened. And the judge ruled in her favor," he told the television station KITV.

And in an October 31, 2005, statement to reporters following his conviction, Fox said, "I vigorously fought the charges against me, which I hold to be untrue. I lost. I believe the people of Waikiki, Ala Moana, and Kakaako deserve to be represented by someone unclouded by a conviction such as the one I now carry."

But according to court transcripts, Galen basically admitted that he'd conducted himself like the national celebrity spokesman for roofies. Then again, for some reason he thought the woman was awake when his arm and leg pressed against her arm and leg, and he interpreted her lack of response as meaning she was "interested in some physical contact."

Wrote the *Star-Bulletin*: "Then, according to his testimony, about 20 minutes or a half hour later, 'I put my hand on her thigh downward. And, then, I turned it very deliberately upward, inviting her to essentially place her hand in my hand.'"

As for the intentional-crotch-rubbing portion of the program, which, let's face it, makes all his other statements seem kind of off-topic, the esteemed legislator was surprisingly candid.

When asked by the judge, "And you did rub her crotch. That was an intentional act?" Fox answered, "Yes."

And just in case you thought that his overture might simply have been part of the brazen, breathless mating dance of two impulsive strangers, torn from the pages of a steamy, bodice-ripping Harlequin novel, the *Star-Bulletin* clarified, "He admitted that the woman did not react or make any sound when he was rubbing her thigh and her crotch area, and that she did not invite his conduct nor give him permission to touch her."

Ultimately, Fox was convicted of abusive sexual conduct and was sentenced to three months of house arrest, three years probation, and "either psychiatric evaluation or sex offender treatment."

One can only hope the first day of treatment included a group discussion on how to avoid contact with previously unacquainted genitalia on trans-Pacific flights.

4.

The Arkansas Family-Values Divorcee

Common Name:
Tim Hutchinson

Distinguishing Behaviors:
Spouse-dumping;
Bible-thumping

Distinctive Call:
Sanctimonious wail

In 1996, Arkansas senator Tim Hutchinson, responding to an Associated Press questionnaire, cited "the breakdown of the American family" as one of the two biggest problems facing the country.

The other, apparently, was his wife.

In August 1999, Hutchinson, a Baptist minister by trade, 86'ed the broad he'd been biblically knowin' for nearly three decades, receiving a divorce decree just six days before his 29th wedding anniversary.

"There have been tremendous strains on our marriage during the past few years and we sought extensive counseling prior to taking this action," said Hutchinson in a statement.

Of course, Hutchinson was not your average family-values poseur.

According to the *Arkansas Democrat-Gazette,* "As a state representative, he sponsored home-schooling legislation, sued the state to halt the distribution of contraceptives in school-based health clinics, and signed petitions to impanel a Benton County grand jury to investigate the distribution of obscene videos.

"He received a Friend of the Family Award from the Christian Coalition for an 'outstanding record in support of family values.'"

But while a Baptist minister from Arkansas seeking a divorce from his wife of 29 years may seem like a shocker, it actually fits quite neatly with what science knows about both Baptists and Arkansans.

Arkansas consistently has one of the highest divorce rates in the country (compared to the ultraliberal, gay-magnet den of sin and dark, soul-sucking portal to the underworld, Massachusetts, which consistently has one of the lowest).

Moreover, according to a 1999 survey by the atheist-humanist—or no, that's a typo—the Christian Barna Research Group, Baptists have among the highest divorce rates in the country, with 29 percent having thrown at least one spouse under the matrimonial bus. For the general population the number was 25 percent. Atheists and agnostics clocked in at 21 percent, tied with Catholics and Lutherans. Born-again Christians also helped to blow the curve, coming in at 27 percent.

But despite being just another Christian conservative cliché, Hutchinson lost the 2002 election to Democrat Mark Pryor. However, a Zogby survey taken just two days after the election suggested that his divorce wasn't a big deal to most voters.

Asked about the influence Hutchinson's divorce had on their vote, 12 percent of respondents said it caused them to vote against him, 83 percent said it had no effect, and, for some unfathomable reason that probably only makes sense to Southern Baptists, 3 percent said it caused them to vote for him.

About a year after divorcing, Hutchinson married a former aide. She was quite a bit younger than he. But you probably figured that out all on your own.

5.

Neil Bush: The Mysterious Asian Lady Bushwhacker

Common Name:
Neil Bush

Mating Grounds:
Asian hotel rooms

Distinctive Behavior:
Accidental mating

Embarrassing presidential siblings are part of an august tradition that goes back decades.

From Billy Carter to Roger Clinton to Sam Houston Johnson, first brothers have proven time and again the old adage that some people are born to greatness, others have greatness thrust upon them, and still others have livers the size of Victorian end tables.

But no one has excelled in the first-brother boob-fest like George W. Bush's little sib Neil. While it's scary to think that George may have gotten the brains in the family, looking at Neil's track record it's hard to draw any other conclusion.

Indeed, as callow as George W. is, the nation can take solace in knowing that we were a high-profile savings-and-loan scandal and a modest RV-load of Asian prostitutes away from Neil entering public life.

In 2003, in an improbable narrative that forever lowered the bar for amateur porn directors and *Penthouse Forum* letter writers everywhere, Neil claimed in a deposition that, on several different occasions, women unexpectedly showed up at the door of his hotel room to have sex with him while he was visiting Hong Kong and Thailand on business in the late '90s.

In testimony sought by Neil's ex-wife Sharon's attorney, Neil displayed the wide-eyed bemusement of a lost child who'd just had several Asian prostitutes appear at his door for no reason.

When asked by Sharon's lawyer, Marshall Davis Brown, about possible extramarital dalliances, Neil fessed up to three or four occasions when mysterious women appeared out of the blue to rescue him from his long, bitter, Asian-prostitute-free solitude.

"Mr. Bush, you have to admit that it's a pretty remarkable thing for a man just to go to a hotel room door and open it and have a woman standing there and have sex with her," said Brown.

"It was very unusual," acknowledged Bush.

When Brown asked if the women were prostitutes, Bush answered, "I don't know." When asked if he paid them, Bush admitted he had not.

Now, there are some people who go their entire lives without having a Hong Kong prostitute unexpectedly show up at their door even once, so it would be pretty remarkable if there weren't more to this story.

Indeed, the explanation may—*may*—have something to do with Neil's relationship with Grace Semiconductor Manufacturing Corp., which he was representing on these trips.

Bush was a consultant for the company, which counted among its backers the son of former Chinese president Jiang Zemin. In 2002, Bush signed a deal that paid him $2 million in the company's stock over five years for attending board meetings and discussing business strategies.

"Now, you have absolutely no educational background in semiconductors, do you Mr. Bush?" Brown asked in the deposition.

"That's correct," answered Bush.

While Neil's involvement with the failed Silverado Savings & Loan in the late '80s probably scuttled any political ambitions he may have had, his Far East adventures had to have further embarrassed his family. Indeed, he remains the only member of the Bush family ever to admit having sex with numerous Asian women who may or may have not been harlots.

But the story gets even weirder. After Neil e-mailed his wife to tell her he wanted a divorce, she hired a PR consultant who announced that Sharon Bush planned to write a book about the Bushes. The publicist then arranged a meeting between Sharon and notorious biographer Kitty Kelley.

"I learned a great deal about the Bush family from Sharon," Kelley said in an interview with the *Washington Post*. "She told me he's only offering $1,000 a month in support—take it or leave it. . . . She said that when she told Neil she needs more to live on, Neil Bush said, 'Just get remarried.' Sharon was sobbing as she told me, 'Kitty, I just won't sell my body!'"

Later, John Spalding, a friend of Neil's, told reporters that Sharon had pulled hair from Neil's head so she could make a voodoo doll with which to curse her husband. (Sharon admitted to the hair pulling but claimed it was for a drug test.)

Then Robert Andrews, the ex-husband of Maria Andrews, to whom Neil became romantically linked, filed a defamation suit against Sharon, asking for $850,000 in damages and alleging that Sharon had spread a rumor that Neil had fathered the Andrews' son to reporters, friends, and "fast-food restaurant employees."

This upper-class *Springer* episode did have a happy ending, however. In March of 2004, Neil married Maria Andrews.

DIDJAKNOW?

Both former president George H. W. Bush and former Florida governor Jeb Bush have publicly denied rumors of extramarital affairs.

During the 1992 presidential campaign, the elder Bush called a report in the *New York Post* of a 1984 affair with a female aide "a lie," angrily responding to reporters who asked him about the story. At one point he responded to NBC's Stone Phillips, "You're perpetuating the sleaze by even asking the question, to say nothing of asking it in the Oval Office."

In May 2001, the younger Bush denied rumors of an affair with a political appointee and former Playboy bunny, saying "I cannot tell you how hurtful this is. . . . I love my wife. There is nothing to this rumor. It is an outright lie."

6.

The Oregonian Ass-Grabbin' Packwooder

Common Name:
Bob Packwood

Native Habitat:
Staffers' underpants

Natural Defense:
Able to comouflage
self as champion
and defender of
women

In the long, hallowed history of congressional impropriety, few were as improper as Bob Packwood, the notorious Oregon senator who in a distinguished 27-year Senate career grabbed more staff than Gandalf.

In the fine Republican tradition of recording insanely damaging information for no apparent reason, Packwood kept a diary during his congressional tenure in which he detailed his numerous trysts with young women in his employ.

Now, this wasn't a case of a scorned mistress or two who set out to bring down a powerful lawmaker. No, no. He was the Gandhi of inappropriate ass-grabbing.

One diary entry reportedly referred to "the 22 staff members I'd made love to and probably 75 others I've had passionate relationships with."

Another talked of an encounter with a young woman in his office. "[We] made love, and she has the most stunning figure—big breasts . . . I rather enjoyed it in the sense that it wasn't wham-bam-thank-you-ma'am," he wrote.

But while office romances between bosses and subordinates are always tricky, you can't expect to cast this wide a net without snaring a pissed-off shark or two.

While Packwood apparently had sex with many women, he also apparently harassed many as well. Indeed, before all was said and done, the Senate Select Committee on Ethics, which had looked into the sexual harassment allegations, released 10,145 pages of evidence it had collected against him. It included 111 depositions taken from 264 witnesses and weighed 40 pounds, or as much as the mystery grandchild who should be knocking on his door any day now. In all, at least 17 women alleged unwanted sexual advances over a period of 11 years.

Now, few are so naive as to believe that Capitol Hill doesn't boast more than its share of sexual impropriety, but this was just greedy. No doubt many, if not most, Washington power brokers have tried to get into the pants of a coworker at one time or another, but they're not trying to keep pace with the local Blue Cross Blue Shield OB/GYN directory.

Fellow Republican Mitch McConnell, who chaired the Ethics Committee, summed it up best.

"These were not merely stolen kisses, as Senator Packwood has claimed," he said. "There was a habitual pattern of aggressive, blatantly sexual advances, mostly directed at members of his own staff or others whose livelihoods were connected in some way to his power and authority as a Senator."

Packwood eventually resigned in September 1995, three years after the case first came to light in a November 1992 *Washington Post* story.

To put it in perspective, he was on the verge of being the first member to be expelled from the Senate since the Civil War. So while what he did was not necessarily as bad as standing in open rebellion against the legitimate government of the United States to preserve a morally repellent, slave-based aristocracy that vividly represented repression, brutal tyranny, and savage injustice, it was apparently in the ballpark.

The whole Packwood affair originally took many by surprise,

given the senator's reputation as a champion of women. The lengthy 1992 *Washington Post* story that first exposed Packwood led with this same apparent contradiction:

"Ask those who have worked for Sen. Bob Packwood about his treatment of women, and two portraits emerge.

"One is the Oregon Republican's record as a leading advocate of women's rights during his 24 years in the Senate and his much-admired history of hiring women, promoting them and supporting their careers even after they leave his office. Women currently hold the most powerful posts on his staff."

Okay, so maybe that doesn't quite exonerate him. It's kind of like saying John Wayne Gacy must have been innocent because he performed as a clown at children's parties.

The story would go on, of course, to detail Packwood's treatment of the many women he hired.

One story recounted Packwood's advances toward a young staffer who held a low-level position in his office:

"In early 1976, [a 21-year-old woman was a] college graduate with a new job as a mail clerk in Packwood's Washington office. At the bottom of the staff hierarchy, she was surprised when Packwood invited her into his office once to play bridge with two top aides, she recalled in recent interviews. Soon after, Packwood buzzed her on the interoffice phone and asked her to come to his office.

"She said Packwood locked the door behind her and then embraced her, running his fingers through her hair and forcefully kissing her on the lips. She said he told her how much he liked her wholesome good looks. 'It was very clear that it was a sexual thing,' she said. 'It was very hard to get him to let go of me.'

"[The woman] said she pulled away and talked her way out of his office. After the incident, she said, a Packwood aide told her that such advances had occurred before and advised her not to go into his office alone. [She] said she ignored two more invitations from Packwood to come to his office. Within a few months, she said, she took another Capitol Hill position."

The Senate Ethics Counsel would eventually release a "best of" collection of Packwood's peccadilloes, titled *The Packwood Report,* shortly after Packwood resigned. It's still available at online retailers.

In his farewell address, Packwood summed up his career as only he could.

"There have been many successes in these 27 years, some failures, some frustrations," he said.

Oh, Bob. There can be no doubt.

7.

The White-Robed Buckeye Buz

Common Name:
Buz Lukens

Distinctive Plumage:
Terry cloth

Bird Song:
"Love in an
Elevator"

Next Thursday, July 20, will be an historic day for America, as America celebrates the 20th anniversary of Neil Armstrong and Buz Luken walking on the moon. . . .
—Dan Quayle, speaking at the Young Republicans National Federation Convention, July 15, 1989

Buz Lukens never walked on the moon. However, he did pay an underage girl for sex. But it's easy to see how Dan Quayle was confused. Lukens and Buzz Aldrin do, after all, have similar names. It happens to the best of us. Think about how many times you've been at a cocktail party and started going on and on about how Walt Whitman's genius was evident in his creation of Mickey Mouse, or how Mama Celeste was your favorite '60s folk singer.

But, for the record, Buz Lukens never walked on the moon. Ever.

Back in 1989, Donald E. "Buz" Lukens was a Republican congressman from Ohio. But in May of that year, he saw the career he'd built starting to slip through his fingers.

A girl, who had been just 16 when Lukens had sex with her, testified against him in his trial on charges of contributing to the delinquency of a minor.

Lukens, like all good conservatives caught with their hand in the cookie jar, proceeded to blame the cookie jar.

But the jury seemed more interested in the victim's testimony. She testified how she had been paid $40 for her services, along with a metal pillbox and a pink lace fan. So not only was Lukens a predator, but he was a cheap one at that.

The girl recounted that on November 6, 1988, she and a friend went to Lukens's apartment, and he answered the door in his underwear.

The girl then stated that Lukens took them to the guest room and "told us to get undressed and put on two black robes." When the girl asked why they couldn't wear the two white robes that were also in the room, "he said those were for white people."

Lukens was convicted of a misdemeanor and sentenced to 30 days in jail. And although Buz Lukens never did walk on the moon, he certainly had the cojones to do it. Even after his conviction, he refused to step down from Congress, despite urging from members of his own party to do so.

Robert T. Bennett, the chairman of the Ohio Republican Party, said, "His offense is so serious that the county chairman of the Eighth District and I are in full agreement that we must disassociate the party from his actions and ask for his resignation from the Republican state committee and the United States Congress."

Oh, but that was by no means the final chapter in the Buz Lukens story.

A year later he finally resigned after being accused of fondling a Capitol elevator operator.

Yeah, maybe we could ship him to the moon after all.

8.

The Easily Duped Steam-Room-Dwelling Pigeon

Common Name:
Andrew Buhr

Distinguishing Characteristics:
Flushed face; dazed expression

Native Habitat:
YMCA steam room

Status:
Roaming free

Paloma Picasso Tiffany & Co. cufflinks you bought when you campaigned as a Republican for a Missouri House seat . . . $225.

Hermes tie you picked up for yourself after receiving a prestigious appointment from the president . . . $148.

Not being able to tell that the guy you're having anal sex with is 14 . . . Priceless.

In his early 30s, Andrew Buhr seemed destined for a bright career in politics. A rising young star in the Missouri Republican Party, he had served as a Republican committeeman for the Hadley Township. And though he lost his 2000 bid for the 84th District Missouri House seat, in November 2002 George W. Bush appointed him to the Commission on Presidential Scholars.

But he would be summarily unappointed less than a month later after charges were filed relating to a December 2001 incident in a men's steam room at the Wildwood, Missouri, YMCA.

In an interview with the St. Louis biweekly newspaper *Vital Voice,* Buhr explained the courtship with the young man who would later prove problematic to his career in politics.

"I was at the gym at the Y and there was no doubt that he was 18 (in my mind) because I met him at the gym and he was in a room with a sign on the door that said you must be 18 or older to be there," Buhr said. "He was a big guy, well over six feet, well over 200 pounds. Plus the fact that it was a steam room where I've met other men there, it wasn't an uncommon thing. His behavior, the conversation about college, he did say he was 18."

In courtroom testimony during Buhr's trial, it was revealed that the teen had suggested the two should find other accommodations. When Buhr asked who should drive, the teen suggested that they use Buhr's car, then directed him to a restroom near the high school. All seemed to be going according to plan as the two traded blowjobs.

On the drive back, Buhr asked the teen where he should drop him off. At that point, the boy told him that his mother would be picking him up.

Ouch.

With a little pressing, the teen finally admitted that he was 16. Then 15. And so on.

At first, Buhr didn't believe him, thinking it was some sort of twisted joke.

"I didn't think someone that young would have all this planned out," he said. "I didn't believe him."

Apparently, the boy had been doing this with a number of men and eventually got royally busted by his parents, who had intercepted a cell phone message from another gentleman caller. An investigation was launched, and Buhr was eventually arrested along with three other men and charged with two counts of statutory sodomy.

While the case made for interesting news coverage, Buhr was ultimately acquitted by a jury in August 2004 after a deadlocked jury had forced a mistrial earlier in the year.

After the second trial, one female jury member said of the teen's behavior, "He obviously had a routine that he had done before."

That may be true, but any good conservative should know that a first date rarely goes well when it starts out in a restroom outside the local high school.

9.

The Dimwitted Quayle with Parkinson's Envy

Common Name:
Thomas Evans/
Dan Quayle

Mating Grounds:
Washington, D.C.,
and any back nine

Distinctive Approach:
Dirty dancing
(alleged)

Every once in a while, out of the putrefying morass of influence peddling and corporate cronyism that is Washington politics, a little integrity slithers out.

Witness former Delaware congressman Thomas Evans. When it came time to mix the ol' baby batter with a female lobbyist who represented key industry interests that were subject to congressional oversight, he was careful to select one who was fighting passage of a bill he already planned on voting against.

Evans was thrust into the national spotlight when it was revealed that lobbyist Paula Parkinson—who would later come to fame for claiming to have shot down the advances of an amorous Dan Quayle—had taken a Florida golf trip in 1980 with Evans, Quayle, and Illinois congressman Tom Railsback.

The attorney general later requested that the Justice Department look into the situation, and it was around this same time when Evans got all weird and defensive and stuff.

According to a story in the *Washington Post:* "Evans reiterated his earlier statement that

Parkinson did not influence his vote on the crop-insurance legislation. He voted against the bill (which passed anyway) not because of her, he said, but because it was 'entirely consistent with my economic philosophy.'"

Yeah, we know what you're thinking. Even the sleaziest of relationships begs for a little more romance than this. Indeed, one can only wonder what kind of a silver-tongued Casanova Evans was in the bedroom:

Parkinson: Oh God, oh God, oh God. Right there. Yes. Oh God.

Evans: Ohhhhh, yes, yes! Oh God. Yes! Right there. Ohhhhhh, you are soooo entirely consistent with my economic philosophy.

Parkinson would also pose for the November 1980 edition of *Playboy,* where she would helpfully confide that "Washington is basically a very horny city." (With all due respect to Parkinson, that's true of pretty much every American city, with the possible exception of the Main Street U.S.A. exhibit at Disneyland.)

In August of 1981, the Justice Department announced that no charges would stem from Parkinson's extracurricular activities, despite, as one source told the *New York Times,* her "salacious accounts of purported activities with congressmen."

And that might have been the end of it, had George H. W. Bush not chosen human highlight reel Dan Quayle as his running mate for the 1988 presidential election.

In the summer of '88, *Playboy* interviewed Parkinson for its November issue, setting off a whirlwind of controversy over who was actually more airbrushed, Parkinson or Quayle.

When asked about rumors of an involvement with Quayle, Parkinson told the magazine that they hadn't had any actual sexual congress.

"He wanted to, but I was there as Tom Evans' date," said Parkinson. "We flirted a lot and danced extremely close and suggestively. He said he wanted to make love." (In fairness to Quayle, when he said he wanted to make love, he may have actually been talking about Marilyn. The man never was one for, you know, speech.)

Parkinson's charges were, of course, met with heated denials. Quayle called the story "an absolute, flat-out falsehood."

"I had nothing to do with her down there," said Quayle. "I think y'all are going to have to be a little careful about this, because it's totally untrue. I've got a wife and three small children, and I hope there's some respect and dignity for things I did not do before we go rushing off with all these so-called rumors."

While "respect and dignity for things I did not do" would have actually been an ideal campaign slogan for the eventual VP, whether or not Quayle nailed more birds than birdies on the trip was quickly fading in importance. His religious conservative base had to have been wondering what in the name of Jesus Herschel Christ he was doing there in the first place.

For his part, Evans, who lost his 1982 reelection bid in large measure because of his association with Parkinson, seemed affronted that anyone would think Quayle was horning in on his wildly inappropriate relationship with a lobbyist. He claimed it was impossible that Parkinson's story about Quayle was true— presumably because he was banging the broad the entire time.

From an August 1988 story in the *Washington Post:*

"Reached last night, Evans, who has acknowledged having had an affair with Parkinson, said it is 'inconceivable' that Quayle could have propositioned the lobbyist. During the long golfing weekend, he said, various members of the group went and returned but Quayle and Parkinson only overlapped a brief time.

"'They were there together just one day and one night, they overlapped just that long,' Evans said. 'There was nothing what-soever between Paula Parkinson and Dan Quayle in Florida, period.'"

Of course, the scandal wasn't enough to sink Quayle's vice-pres-idential prospects. His deft management of the embarrassing crisis would pave the way for many more embarrassments to come— none of which, thankfully, involved any bare-naked lobbyists.

10.
The Helms-Headed Odd-Duck Finkelstein

Common Name:
Arthur J. Finkelstein

Mating Call:
Republican talking points

Distinctive Behavior:
Bizarre hypocrisy

Status:
Gay as a goose

Taking a good look at the pervy political rogue's gallery, it's hard to imagine where the event horizon of outlandish GOP hypocrisy might possibly lie.

Seriously, what would it take for the party to finally implode from the sheer weight of its own contradictions? Someone like Laura Bush turning tricks on K Street for Heritage Foundation fellows while decked out in fishnet stockings, cherry lip gloss, and spandex? Jesse Helms' star campaign strategist marrying a man?

Take, for instance, the case of Arthur J. Finkelstein, the star campaign strategist for Jesse Helms's 1990 Senate run who, in a quiet December 2004 ceremony at his home in Massachusetts, married a man.

"I believe that visitation rights, health care benefits and other human relationship contracts that are taken for granted by all married people should be available to partners," said Finkelstein after announcing it was wedding bells for him and his male partner.

Finkelstein declined to identify his

partner—perhaps so it would be harder for Dick Cheney to use his X-Men Cerebro headgear to locate him—but the love whose name he dare not speak had apparently been with him for forty years and, ostensibly by his side, as he fought to elect candidates who found the devotion the couple shared totally gross and repugnant.

Yes, unless we all missed something and a shirtless, eyebrow-waxed, edible-condom-festooned Jesse Helms danced with Arthur J. Finkelstein to the ebullient strains of "It's Raining Men" at the former's 1990 election-eve victory party, the Fabulous Miss F. has some 'splaining to do.

Indeed, after being outed by *Boston Magazine* in 1996, Finkelstein came under attack by progay groups for representing clients who were, to say the least, not with the program.

In addition to Helms, he had advised George Pataki, who as governor of New York said gay Massachusetts marriages would not be recognized there. And he once conducted a poll for Mormon Mitt Romney prior to his successful 2002 run for Massachusetts governor. (Romney opposes gay marriage, presumably because the magical golden disks he found inside his lettuce crisper told him to.)

Naturally, Finkelstein's political opponents were puzzled by the revelation. It would be like the head of the House Caucus on Missing and Exploited Children . . . okay, never mind.

"He's a hypocrite," said Philip W. Johnston, Massachusetts Democratic Party chair. "For years he's worked for right-wing candidates who demonize gays and lesbians, and who have tried to prevent gays and lesbians from being married."

Even Bill Clinton, whose wife was to be the focus of a 2006 campaign orchestrated by Finkelstein, threw down.

"Either this guy believes his party is not serious and he's totally Machiavellian," said Clinton, or "he may be blinded by self-loathing."

However, at least one of Finkelstein's friends, Michael McKeon, a fellow Republican strategist, tried to deflect the hypocrisy charge back onto Clinton.

"It's really beneath a former president to comment on someone's personal life like that," McKeon told the *New York Times*. "After everything he has been through in his own life, you'd think he'd know better."

Now, Bill Clinton was no saint, as we all know, but McKeon's hypocrisy charge would only hold up if the former president were stumping for candidates whose key campaign issue was opposing blow jobs from Monica Lewinsky.

Face it, if you're gay, you shouldn't be refurbishing Jesse Helms's new kitchen, much less getting him reelected.

11.

The Domino-Effect Molesting South Carolinian Russell

Common Name:
Beverly Russell

Native Habitat:
Christian Coalition
and Citizens for
Life offices

*Distinguishing
Behavior:*
Molesting his
stepdaugher

In November of 1994, Susan Smith, a South Carolina mother, famously confessed to drowning her three-year-old son Michael and fourteen-month-old son Alex by strapping them into her car and letting it roll into a local lake.

It was seen as a national tragedy, and observers struggled to make sense of it.

But while trying to tease out the sociological, psychological, and biochemical intricacies of such a story might have seemed daunting to some—particularly those without intimate knowledge of the case—Newt Gingrich apparently had insight into infanticide that had eluded the Western world since time immemorial.

In an interview just prior to the 1994 midterm elections, Gingrich said, "I think that the mother killing the two children in South Carolina vividly reminds every American how sick the society is getting and how much we need to change things," Gingrich said. "The only way you get change is to vote Republican."

He later referred to a "direct nexus between the general acceptance of violence" and "the pattern that the counterculture and Lyndon Johnson's Great Society began in the late '60s."

Of course, he could have just as easily blamed the Whig Party and the deeply unsettling works from Thomas Kinkade's blue period and he would have been about as accurate.

Turns out, Susan Smith had been molested by her stepfather, Beverly Russell, from the age of fifteen. And as Russell served as county chairman of the Christian Coalition and county coordinator of the South Carolina Citizens for Life, his twisted relationship with his stepdaughter continued. Russell would also sit on the state Republican Party's executive committee.

In fact, Smith claimed her father once molested her after he'd been out putting up Pat Robertson for President signs (which, to be honest, is a lateral move at best).

While Russell's guilt was not in question—he had admitted to the touching in court records that were unsealed after Smith killed her children, and during her trial confessed to having sexual relations with her until just months before the drownings—it was still unclear whether Smith's murders should be pinned on Russell, Head Start, or the Voting Rights Act of 1965.

Let's just call it a draw.

12.
The Amazing Anti–Sex Ed Adulterer

You could say that Mary Kay Letourneau was to screwing teenage students what Niels Bohr was to quantum light theory—a pioneer in the field who was not quite as slutty as those who came after him.

And as Bohr was no doubt inspired by the paradigm-shifting work of Einstein and Newton, Letourneau was similarly influenced by her predecessors.

In fact, *her* mentor turned out to be none other than her father, John Schmitz, the erstwhile California lawmaker whose political career was derailed in 1982 after it was revealed that he'd sired two illegitimate children by a woman who had been his student at Santa Ana College.

Now Schmitz, who served in the U.S. Congress and the California state senate, was not your run-of-the-mill conservative. Imagine for a moment the official Republican platform with the added planks of "Keeping Sex Education Out of Schools" and "Giving Joe McCarthy his due." That'll give you an inkling of just how far-right Schmitz really was.

Indeed, Schmitz was so conservative he:

- Was asked to leave the John Birch Society because his extreme comments supposedly hurt the group's reputation. (Which is a little like getting fired from T.G.I. Friday's for being too peppy.)
- Said, "I'm only opposed to him coming back" when asked whether he opposed Richard Nixon's famous 1972 trip to China.
- Once chaired a committee hearing on abortion, prompting his office to issue a press release headlined, "Senator Schmitz and His Committee Survive Attack of the Bulldykes." The release claimed the hearing's audience had "hard, Jewish, and arguably female faces."
- Purchased the home of Senator Joe McCarthy, his hero.
- In 1972, ran against Richard Nixon for president on a fringe-party ticket.
- Was vehemently opposed to sex education. (According to LeTourneau's lawyer, David Gehrke, Schmitz was so opposed to sex education, he'd pull his daughter out of a school if there was any indication that they were considering it. As a child in California, she went from one Catholic school to another "because they kept getting too liberal," said Gehrke.)

Of course, while sex education in the classroom was a big taboo for Schmitz, sex itself was apparently another story.

Schmitz once wrote, in his 1974 book *Stranger in the Arena,* that we are not "free to break the Ten Commandments . . . to lie, to covet . . . to commit adultery."

That, of course, was before his secret mistress and two illegitimate children were revealed to the world. For some reason, people noticed the inconsistency, and his subsequent 1984 congressional bid failed, as being a good family man is generally not interpreted as meaning you should have a spare one.

Sometime after Letourneau's legal troubles (i.e. being imprisoned for child rape after having a baby with a thirteen-year-old student) were made public, Schmitz threw in his two cents. Well, actually, a ha'penny would have to do. He blamed liberals.

"No one has used the argument that statutory rape, at least according to the Blackstone [law] dictionary, was solely a crime that a man could commit," said Schmitz.

"It would seem to me that it became a woman's crime when you had this political egalitarianism, which has led to Washington state's having an equal-rights amendment, although it was rejected by the United States. That makes this a very political case.

"I was one of the leading opponents of the Equal Rights Amendment when I was in the Congress."

Schmitz is now annoying both God and Nixon over their flaming liberal ways. He died in 2001 after nearly 70 years of uninterrupted crazy talk.

13.
The Gang-Bangin' Well-Pumped Governator

Common Name:
Arnold Schwarzenegger

Desired Mates:
Liberal chicks from great American families or any other babes who happen to be in the room

Distinctive Behavior:
Group sex

The infamous 2003 California recall election answered once and for all two eternal mysteries: (1) How many people in our nation's most populous state are stupid enough to hand the reins of the government presiding over one of the ten largest economies in the world to the second lead in *Red Sonja?**And (2) How many allegations of unwanted sexual contact does it take before your poll numbers finally start to sink below Gary Coleman's?

The answer to both questions? Lots.

Just days before the October 2003 election, the *Los Angeles Times* ran a story in which six women alleged they had been groped by action film star and former bodybuilder Arnold Schwarzenegger in separate incidents from 1975 to 2000. A few days later, as California voters prepared to go to the polls, the number of women alleging groping incidents grew to fifteen.

---

*Then again, some would argue that Gray Davis could have only dreamed of being the second lead in *Red Sonja.*

Apparently realizing that trying to keep a lid on his lecherous past would have been a little like Michael Caine denying that he'd been in *Jaws 4,* Schwarzenegger made a confession of sorts after the first *Times* story ran.

"Wherever there is smoke, there is fire," Schwarzenegger said as he prepared to tour the state in his appropriately named bus "Predator." "I have done things that were not right, which I thought then was playful, but now I recognize that I have offended people."

Well, "playful" may not be quite the right word. Indeed, there's a reason there was very little tit-grabbing in *Kindergarten Cop.* It doesn't go over well with the female over-40 demo.

Of course, there was plenty of smoke before the *LA Times* outed him.

For instance, a 1977 interview with Schwarzenegger in *Oui* magazine recalled a disturbing incident at a California gym.

"There was a black girl who came out naked," Schwarzenegger said. "Everyone jumped on her and took her upstairs, where we all got together."

When asked if he was referring to a "gang bang," Schwarzenegger said, "Yes, but not everybody, just the guys who can fuck in front of other guys. Not everybody can do that. Some think that they don't have a big-enough cock, so they can't get a hard-on."

Granted, that answer was eerily similar to at least one exchange from Princess Diana's famous BBC interview with Martin Bashir, but that didn't diminish its crudity.

A 2001 article in *Premiere*, titled "Arnold the Barbarian," alleged that Schwarzenegger had fondled the breasts of both a female crew worker and his *Terminator 2* costar Linda Hamilton. (Hamilton later denied the incident had taken place.)

And in a 2003 interview with *Esquire*, Schwarzenegger showed his evolution from lunkheaded boor to fuzzy-sweatered Phil Donahue feminist, saying, "As much as when you see a blonde with great tits and a great ass, you say to yourself, 'Hey, she must be stupid or must have nothing else to offer,' which maybe is the case many times. But then again, there is the one that is as smart as her breasts look, great as her face looks, beautiful as her whole body looks gorgeous, you know, so people are shocked."

While Schwarzenegger's political ambitions were not impeded by his past, the allegations hounded him until August of 2006, when he settled a libel suit brought against him by Anna Richardson, a British former TV host who had claimed that, during a taped interview, Arnold pulled her toward him and squeezed her nipple.

Richardson later claimed Schwarzenegger's people said she had encouraged the behavior.

Yeah, she didn't like that much. Grabbing the boob was probably the worse call, but the campaign's response probably came in a close second.

14.

The Great Southern Segregationist Intermingler

Common Name:
Strom Thurmond

Distinguishing Behaviors:
Inveighing against race-mixing

Distinguishing Characteristics:
Extremely white

Status:
Extinct

It's been said that blood is thicker than water. Or, in the case of Strom Thurmond's now-famous African American daughter, blood is thicker than whatever happened to be running through the senator's veins there at the end—most likely embalming fluid, catacomb dust, and a few lingering red blood cells his doctors had taken the trouble to individually name.

In 2003, Essie Mae Washington-Williams announced that she was the daughter of the powerful former segregationist senator and the Thurmond family maid.

Thurmond, who earlier in 2003 had finally decided to make his death official, had never formally acknowledged Washington-Williams, though after the announcement the Thurmond family did.

Essie-Mae's mother was naive, 16, and black—and Thurmond a 22-year-old, still reasonably moist old-guard Southerner years away from running for president as a staunch segregationist—when his lordly seed found purchase within her.

Washington-Williams held her tongue for 78 years before letting the world know that the man who once assured his constituency that "on the question of social intermingling of the races, our people draw the line" had done a little intermingling of his own.

Still, Thurmond wasn't a complete cad, which may be why Washington-Williams handled her announcement with what could only be described as remarkable restraint and dignity.

As the *New York Times* wrote when the news of Thurmond's 78-year-old papoose finally came out, "Despite rumors of an illegitimate black child that shadowed Mr. Thurmond for decades, and occasional published reports that named her, he never acknowledged Ms. Washington-Williams as anyone more than a friend.

"And while outsiders were always left to guess in hushed tones the nature of their relationship, [Washington-Williams's attorney Frank K.] Wheaton said, 'it was never a secret' in the Thurmond family and his staff that the woman who saw him nearly every year on one coast or the other was his daughter."

Of course, a 100-year-old former segregationist Republican senator from South Carolina hangin' with a random 78-year-old black woman as a "friend" is bound to raise eyebrows. One would naturally have to wonder what the basis of that friendship could possibly be, and where they might have become acquainted. A *Gilmore Girls* fans chatroom?

While Washington-Williams's handling of the relationship was admirable—she came forward at the urging of her children after her father's death only to establish family history, and made no claim on the Thurmond estate—it's almost a shame that the two hadn't gone public earlier. It would have almost certainly made for the best reality show ever.

Still, Washington-Williams did eventually write a book. In 2006, she released *Dear Senator: A Memoir by the Daughter of Strom Thurmond*.

While taking on the inherent contradictions and difficulties of being a black woman with a secret, virulently antisegregationist father who simply would not fucking die, Washington-Williams, who would have had every excuse to be bitter, nevertheless cut the man some slack: "I knew he loved my mother. I believed he loved me, after his fashion," she wrote.

In a review in the *Buffalo News,* staff reporter Charity Vogel called the book "classy and eye-opening" and wrote that "throughout her tale, Washington-Williams resists any dips into sensationalism, voyeurism or sleaze."

As tempting as it might be to imagine Strom Thurmond's naked body in a sweaty clinch with the girl who scrubbed his underpants, you would be well advised to do the same.

15.

The Web-Surfin', Man-Lovin'
Antigay Spokanian

Common Name:
Jim West

Mating Grounds:
ClosetedSpokaneMayors.
com

*Distinguishing
Behavior:*
Giving really lame
analogies

*Distinctive
Characteristic:*
Most likely to get
interviewed by and
simultaneously want
to bone Matt Lauer

In 1990, former Washington state senator and Spokane mayor Jim West sponsored a bill to make sexual contact for anyone under the age of 18 illegal.

Four years earlier, he had cosponsored a bill to bar gays from teaching in public schools or working in daycare centers, and had remained an opponent of gay rights throughout his political career.

Yeah, you don't exactly have to be Sigmund Freud to figure out the rest.

In May of 2005, Spokane's *Spokesman-Review* published a series of articles alleging West's sexual crimes and misdemeanors.

Most troubling were the allegations by two men that West had molested them when he was a Boy Scout leader and Spokane County sheriff's deputy during the '70s.

West vehemently denied those charges, saying, "I didn't abuse them. I don't know these people. I didn't abuse anybody, and I didn't have sex with anybody under 18—ever—woman or man."

But the newspaper's other major allegation—

that West had "used the trappings of the mayor's office to entice and influence young men he met on a gay Web site"—was harder to dismiss. The paper had transcripts.

"On one recent occasion, West offered a man he believed to be an 18-year-old—whom he met online at Gay.com—gifts, favors, and a city hall internship, Internet dialogues retained by the newspaper reveal," the *Spokesman-Review* reported. "The 18-year-old was actually a forensic computer expert working for the newspaper."

Actually, the undercover expert had initially claimed to be 17 when the chats began in February, but later told West he would turn 18 in March. It was after he supposedly turned 18 that the two talked about meeting.

So, suddenly finding himself caught in a web of contradictions stickier than his Haley Joel Osment mouse pad, West struggled to explain away his behavior.

In a profile in the *New York Times,* he claimed the Internet was a seductive fantasy outlet:

"It allowed you to say things that you might not say otherwise because of that fantasy element, because of that anonymity element, because of the private element of it all," he said. "Do you recall the game Dungeons & Dragons that kids got all sucked into? It was kind of that—curiosity—and then you get sucked in and then you just converse with people and it's role-playing almost."

Yeah, except when kids played D&D, the dungeon master was not literally a dungeon master and a +2 Elven bag of holding was not something you did in a park restroom between police and fire commission meetings.

In a May 2005 interview with *Today's* Matt Lauer, West also addressed the apparent hypocrisy of struggling against gay rights while simultaneously struggling to get into more than one gay's pants.

(According to the *Spokesman-Review,* West had consistently opposed expanded civil rights protections for gays when it came to housing and employment and voted for a statewide ban on gay marriage in 1998.)

Lauer: The one issue is that we have a mayor who was out-spoken opposing gay rights.

West: Not necessarily, Matt. You know, I voted to repre-sent my legislative district in the legislature. I was not an advocate, I did not stand up, I was not a leader of the charge in any of those cases. Every representative and every senator from my district has voted exactly the way I voted at some time.

Lauer: So you're saying this was purely politics. This—this was business.

West: Representative government. When people elect you to go to the legislature, they elect you to do—to do certain things, representative government. My district votes that way.

Lauer: But did you ever—did you ever say, Mr. Mayor, that when you were voting against some of these bills that would have given more rights to gay couples, for example, and yet you were visiting gay chat sites and having relation-ships with men, did you ever in your private time say, "Man, this is hypocritical'?

West: You know, Matt, somebody explained it to me this way just about a week ago, and they said, "If, if you hire somebody to paint your house blue, and they think it ought to look better red, what color do you want your house to be painted?" The people of my legislative district elected all the representatives and all the senators to go to Olympia and represent them. And the majority of the people in my district, that's the way they feel.

Well, never mind, then.

In December 2005, West was recalled by voters. He died of complications from surgery in July 2006. Sadly, the rest of us have to live on with this story eternally tattooed on our minds.

16.

The Alleged Mistress-Choking Pennsylvania Sherwood

Common Name:
Don Sherwood

Native Habitat:
Small-town America

Distinctive Behavior:
Alleged choking
(unconfirmed)

Distinguishing Characteristics:
Rosy cheeks; big glasses

In the fall of 2006, as her husband, Don, fought for his political life in the midst of a high-profile scandal, Carol Sherwood took the time to scold the congressman's midterm election opponent:

"Chris Carney might be trying to make himself look squeaky clean, but we have all made mistakes we regret over the years," she wrote in a letter to voters. "I am certainly not condoning the mistake Don made, but I'm not going to dwell on it, either."

Well, this may be kind of obvious, but when your opponent admits to a five-year affair with a woman less than half his age, who at one point accused him of trying to choke her and later filed a $5.5 million civil suit against him alleging repeated physical abuse, your campaign strategy is not going to focus on the man's attendance record. At that juncture it's generally considered acceptable form to respond to every one of your opponent's debate points with a question about the best places to find Italian food near the Capitol.

To illustrate just exactly how much trouble Sherwood was in during his reelection battle, he invited George W. Bush, who in October of 2006 was polling roughly as well as spinach, to campaign with him in Pennsylvania.

Saying he was "deeply moved" by Carol Sherwood's comments, Bush said, "Carol's letter shows what a caring and courageous woman she is."

Yeah, when your best applause line is about how awesome the wife of the accused strangler who cheated on her is, you're pretty much just visiting Pennsylvania for the free chocolate and Amish tail.

Sherwood's career first started to nosedive in September of 2004 when his mistress, Cynthia Ore, called 911 and claimed he tried to choke her. Sherwood denied the incident.

Then, in June of 2005, Ore filed a lawsuit against Sherwood, alleging he had "repeatedly and violently physically assaulted and abused" her while the affair was ongoing.

Sherwood admitted to the affair but denied the abuse, saying, "I will defend myself to the fullest extent possible against these malicious and baseless allegations, which in large part have already been fully investigated and rejected by law enforcement officials."

The two later settled the suit for what the Associated Press reported was $500,000.

But it apparently wasn't always so contentious between the two accidental lovers, who first got acquainted at an event for young Republicans in 1999.

"We had such good chemistry," said Ore in an interview with the *Wilkes-Barre (Pennsylvania) Times Leader*. "I saw Don as a small-town all-American. He has that pink, rosy skin. When I first met him, he had those big glasses."

Yes, married 60-somethings with violent tempers who match the precise physical description of Harry Caray can be tough for any blushing young ingénue to pass up, but one wonders where exactly Ore thought the relationship was going.

In one of the least shocking results of the 2006 midterm

elections, Sherwood lost his seat to Carney, a Navy Reserve lieutenant commander who, as far as anyone knew, had yet to conduct a lengthy affair with a woman half his age.

17.

The Quintuple-Marrying, Once-Affronted Seminole County Stelling

Common Name:
Jim Stelling

Common Characteristics:
Practices family values

Distinctive Behavior:
Practiced on five wives

One of this nation's core founding principles is the right of every citizen, as guaranteed in our Constitution, to petition the government for a redress of grievances.

Of course, that doesn't mean every lawsuit has equal merit. Indeed, for every *Brown v. Board of Education* there are about twenty scrotum-related civil actions pending at any one time against KitchenAid and John Deere.

The landmark case of *Jim Stelling v. Nancy Goettman* is another case in point.

In May of 2005, Stelling, chairman of the Seminole County, Florida, Republican Party, sued Goettman, a fellow GOPster, over a letter she sent to party leaders claiming that Stelling had been married six times. Stelling said the letter was "unconscionable" and complained that it may have ruined his chance to become state Republican chairman.

"I believe in family values," Stelling told the court.

Stelling had every right to be angry, of course.

He had actually been married just five times.

According to a story in the *St. Petersburg Times:* "The judge prevented Goettman, who served as her own lawyer, from pursuing several lines of questioning, including her attempts to force Stelling to tell the court how many times he has patronized Rachel's, a local strip club." (Who knows, but one could guess at least once per bachelor party, which by itself would make him something of a regular.)

Stelling won the suit over Goettman's letter, which included a spousal abuse claim (ruled false and defamatory), but he received no damages, despite seeking $99,000 plus fees and costs.

Circuit Judge Clayton Simmons apparently believed that erroneously attributing six marriages to a guy like Stelling was a little like trying to defame Steve Guttenberg by telling people he had starred in *Police Academy 5,* and thus ruled that the claim was harmless.

Stelling, on the other hand, was a bit more sanguine about the outcome.

"The lawsuit was about restoring my good name," he said. "I feel like the judge has done that. I feel vindicated."

DIDJAKNOW?

In December 2003, Virginia Senator John Warner married for the third time. He had previously been married to heiress Catherine Mellon and serial wedder Elizabeth Taylor. Both marriages ended in divorce.

18.
The Scandal-Sullied Duke of Cunningham

Common Name:
Randy Cunningham

Also Known as:
"Duke"

Common Behaviors:
Bribe-taking;
alleged prostitute-
patronizing

When it comes to political scandals, you're far worse off being involved in transgressions that people can easily grasp as compared to violations involving the abstruse, shadowy inner workings of government.

For instance, a failed rural real estate venture involving an obscure financial trust company and alleged misuse of executive power doesn't have quite as much resonance as, say, finding out that your congressman cruised East Village gay bars on Easter Sunday while receiving a series of golden showers that rivaled the sprinkler system at Yankee Stadium.

So what about California Republican Randy "Duke" Cunningham resigning from Congress after pleading guilty to taking more than $2 million in bribes, and being sentenced to eight years in prison?

Well, unless he can add a couple centimeters to that cleavage, it's unlikely Fox News and the rest will give it more than a grudging mention.

Oh, but throw a couple of whores into the mix, and now you've got something.

You see, whores are like the marshmallows in a box of Lucky Charms, and we in the media-consuming public are like a bunch of six-year-olds. We eat the somewhat less unhealthy bits because they're there, and because our mothers don't want us to waste, but in the back of our monkey-fist-sized, glucose-besotted brains, we dimly wonder what it would be like to have a cereal that was *nothing but* marshmallows.

And thus, from the faint, sugary mists of long-past Saturday mornings spent in squalid Crunchberry dens, sitting cross-legged and clammy in gnarled, matted hair and vomit-crusted Superfriends jammies, Fox News was born.

Anyway, in April of 2006, the *Wall Street Journal* reported that federal investigators were looking into whether prostitutes were among the items Cunningham received in his congressional graft goodie bag.

Picking up on the story, the *San Diego Union-Tribune* wrote: "A source close to the bribery case, who spoke on condition of anonymity because of the ongoing investigation, told the *Union-Tribune* that Mitchell Wade, who pleaded guilty in February to bribing Cunningham, told federal prosecutors that he periodically helped arrange for a prostitute for the then-congressman.

"A limousine would pick up Cunningham and a prostitute and take them to the ADCS hospitality suite, Wade reportedly told investigators."

Now, you can Google his image and judge for yourself, but while imagining Duke Cunningham (who, in the authors' considered opinion, on a good day looks like a bowl of Quaker oatmeal and on a bad day looks like Duke Cunningham) in any manner of sexual clinch with a vertebrate of any stripe may tax even the most mentally spry among us, this does at least make the story more interesting.

Later, in February 2007, an indictment against Brent Wilkes, an alleged coconspirator in the bribery case, unhappily turned up the unphotogenic Cunningham's name again. Wrote the *New York Times:*

"[T]he indictment charged that Mr. Wilkes paid for a three-day trip to Hawaii in August 2003 on which Mr. Wilkes was accompanied by Mr. Cunningham and an unidentified employee. On the trip, which cost more than $21,000, Mr. Wilkes paid cash for prostitutes, the indictment said, once giving an employee $600 to pay for two prostitutes, tipping one $500."

While it did give a solid frame of reference for what could be a popular party game—"How much would you have to be paid to have sex with Duke Cunningham?"—it wasn't making the disgraced ex-congressman look any better.

For the record, little more is known about the Cunningham prostitution angle. As of this writing, the case against Wilkes was still pending, as, no doubt, is your lunch every time you read the words "Duke Cunningham" and "prostitutes" within twelve paragraphs of each other.

19. The Chatty-Cathy Minnesota Congressman

Common Name:
Arlan Stangeland

Native Habitat:
The land of
10,000 lakes

Unique Behavior:
Speed-dialing hot
female lobbyists

Sometimes you're just caught. You just are.

Your credit card statement turns up six pages of mysterious hotel charges and lingerie purchases. Your mistress has, during your short time together, stored away more DNA samples than the Human Genome Project. The nanny can describe your penis from ninety different angles with electron-microscope precision. You're naked in Chris Hansen's kitchen with a case of Mike's Hard Lemonade in one hand and enough condoms to sheath Liechtenstein in the other.

It's times like these when you have to gut it up, collect whatever scraps of humanity you might have left, and slink away from the public eye, if not the planet.

For some reason, politicians never really see it that way.

For instance, back in 1990, when the world was just a bit more innocent, Minnesota Republican congressman Arlan Stangeland, a father of seven, angrily denied speculation that he might be having an affair.

Saying that his relationship with his suspected

paramour was nothing but professional, Stangeland decried the "vicious rumors and innuendoes" that were being spread about the supposed affair.

And what touched off these "vicious" rumors to begin with? Oh, maybe the "hundreds of phone calls at government expense to a female lobbyist" he made during the '80s, according to the *Washington Post.*

Now, it's possible that Stangeland simply wanted to discuss with the lobbyist the troubling decline of renowned '80s power balladeers REO Speedwagon, or perhaps he had a series of fresh, cutting-edge takes on Imelda Marcos's shoe collection, but, let's face it, it didn't look good.

It's not that it's completely impossible to be a congressman with a female lobbyist friend whom you've called hundreds of times on the public dime without letting things getting weird, but suffice to say, the burden of proof was squarely on him.

Whatever the case, his constituents weren't buying it.

In 1990, after 14 years in office, the public axed Stangeland in favor of Democrat Collin Peterson.

20.
The Red-Faced Bird-Doggin' Nebraska Cornhustler

Common Name:
Pat McPherson

Native Habitat:
Nebraska
burger joints

Status:
Free as a bird

What's worse than being accused of groping a girl in a Red Robin bird costume? Spending $60,000 on your defense—and having your lawyer attempt, unsuccessfully, to raise questions during the trial about the young lady's past sexual conduct. (No doubt "she was dressed like a whore" failed to test well with mock-trial focus groups.)

In February of 2003, Pat McPherson, the Republican election commissioner of Douglas County, Nebraska, stood accused of fondling an oversized Red Robin Gourmet Burgers costume that, unfortunately for him, happened to have a 17-year-old girl inside of it.

According to published reports at the time, the trouble started when a group of VIPs led by McPherson and Omaha City Council president Chuck Sigerson visited Red Robin on the evening of February 7, 2003.

The 4-foot, 7-inch girl, who was given the robin gig because of "her petite size, as well as her sparkling personality," filed a complaint against the men alleging she was assaulted.

In an interview with the *Omaha World-Herald,* the girl's father, who refused to let his daughter be interviewed, claimed that during a visit from the mascot, McPherson stood and leaned against the girl with his cheek on its beak and his hand on its stomach. A member of the party then asked if it was a girl or boy bird, whereupon McPherson allegedly touched the girl's breast with his hand over the costume, declaring it was a girl bird.

When the mascot posed with Sigerson, he allegedly flicked its tail and exposed her underwear.

McPherson was ultimately acquitted by a county judge of third-degree sexual assault and disturbing the peace, while the jury in Sigerson's trial for disturbing the peace failed to reach a unanimous decision. (Prosecutors declined to retry him.)

Still, the impact on McPherson's life read like classic Greek tragedy—or would have, had Oedipus's mother been dressed as a giant cartoon songbird.

McPherson lost his job over the incident and ran up legal bills totaling around $60,000. He said that the total included payments to investigators whom he had hired to work on the case.

Perhaps those investigators contributed to what the *World-Herald* described in an editorial as "unsavory tactics" by McPherson's and Sigerson's attorneys, including the suggestion that the girl was simply looking to cash in on the accusations, and the attempt by McPherson's lawyer, Steve Lefler, to "raise questions about her past sexual conduct."

But it was ultimately McPherson who would attempt to cash in on the incident. In February of 2004, McPherson filed a lawsuit against Red Robin International Inc., alleging "false, wicked and malicious statements" and claiming the restaurant was responsible for the defamation because the girl "acted within the scope of her employment."

Ironically, though, it was his friend's relationship with the restaurant that led to McPherson's Job-like tribulations.

Wrote the *World-Herald:* "The most basic fact is, the entire incident wouldn't have happened if Sigerson had not taken an inappropriate freebie from the restaurant. (Because his dinner had been delayed on a previous visit, restaurant officials offered him transportation in a limousine and free meals for himself and friends.)"

21.

The Adulterous, Comically Hypocritical Kirk

Common Name:
Kirk Fordice

Distinctive Behavior:
Getting a new horse and putting the old one out to pasture while in office

Natural Enemies:
The old horse

There's a natural progression to political sex scandals that mirrors civilization's own progress.

In the ancient world, our leading statesmen and philosophers brutally sodomized children and hosted sex-soaked bacchanals in ornate government palaces.

In the eighteenth century, amid the frenzied flurry of Enlightenment ideas and ideals, they jumped their favorite slaves.

In the early part of the last century, when our nation was poised to reap the full fruits of liberal democracy, they knocked up their maids.

And in the early '90s, they merely got hummers from interns.

So Republican Kirk Fordice, a harsh critic of President Clinton during the latter's twelve-month national time-out for letting the neighbor girl play with his wee-wee, could be forgiven for thinking his affair while governor of Mississippi in the late-'90s was of a much higher order than his ideological rival's.

Indeed, Fordice, who called for Clinton's

resignation and once said, "I think when folks enter public office, they're due all the scrutiny they get," did his best to distinguish his own behavior from the former president's.

Amid charges of hypocrisy over Fordice's open affair with former girlfriend Ann Creson, Fordice said, "I have never lied before a grand jury, never lied to the people, wagging my finger on TV, never conducted a scurrilous affair with a person half my age in the White House in the middle of the day while talking on the telephone to a senator."

Then again, Clinton ultimately kept his marriage together, while Fordice, an advocate of strong family values, openly sought a divorce from his wife of more than forty years, which his wife, Pat, at least initially refused to give him.

Indeed, in a series of statements in June of 1999 that comprised the funniest displays of marital discord since Andy Capp first spun heritable, soul-crushing poverty and booze-fueled domestic violence into comic gold, the Fordices pulled off their best Mark Foley impression—appearing to be on more than one page at the same time.

After the governor's attorney said the couple had hired separate lawyers to work on the details of their divorce, claiming they had been "estranged for a long period of time," that he had "developed a close relationship with a longtime friend, Ann G. Creson," and that he "plans to marry her," Pat Fordice responded through her own attorney.

Her statement said she did not join him during his announcement because, "She was afraid if she did so, it would send the wrong message, i.e., that she has condoned or forgiven her husband's conduct."

It later continued with "Mrs. Fordice feels that she has been caught up in a whirlwind of controversy which she had hoped to avoid for the sake of her children and for the sake of the people of this state, and that it is not fair for Governor Fordice to call upon her to calm the storms by making or adopting public announcements which run contrary to her true feelings."

She then got downright icy: "Mrs. Fordice has not sought out a podium or a public forum to condemn her husband, and she is still hopeful that she will not be put in that position, but only time and his actions—not his words—will tell."

Later that same month, after Kirk Fordice had said his marriage was so beyond repair there were "no communications whatsoever," Pat Fordice flatly contradicted Kirk's characterization of their marriage, conceding only that it was "terribly strained these last $2^1/_2$ years because of outside influences and that other woman."

Of course, one could assume her intention was to continue squeezing his balls to a shade of blue that exists only in God's imagination until such time as their mutual public service was officially terminated:

"Mr. Fordice apparently wants the first lady to grant him a divorce on his terms, which have not even been made known to her, while ushering her out of the mansion in spite of her continued stated desire to continue her service to the people of this state at a time when a measure of integrity and dignity desperately needs to be restored to the office which she and her husband have held as governor and first lady."

Translation: If Pat Fordice happens to be on your Yahoo! Personals list, you might want to think again.

In December of 1999, the *New York Times* reported that, despite Pat Fordice's earlier refusal to leave the governor's mansion, she had "negotiated herself 'a very favorable agreement,'" and was "headed for a new life in a new home."

The Fordices divorced in 2000, and Kirk died in September 2004, just four years after leaving office.

22.
The Eastern Minnesota Partying Grunseth

Common Name:
Jon Grunseth

Distinguishing Features:
Amphibious; possibly ambidextrous

Natural Enemies:
Eccentric incumbents; curious reporters

Habitat:
Definitely not the Minnesota governor's mansion

Minnesota's Jon Grunseth should have had a pretty good shot at the governor's mansion in 1990.

After all, his opponent, incumbent Rudy Perpich, who was serving his second term as governor, was by all accounts something of an eccentric.

A 1977 profile on Perpich in the *Washington Post* described some of his more off-kilter behavior: "In his seven months as governor, Perpich has been unpredictable, open almost to a fault, and, at times, outrageous.

"At various points, he's banned the pickup of litter along state highways, ordered that a $17,500 increase in his salary be used to buy Italian bocce balls, thrown away a prepared speech when he found the crowd would rather see him polka, dined with Minneapolis' best-known madam, and slipped away from his office alone and unannounced to mingle with farmers and small town businessmen."

But there's a hard-and-fast rule among old-school political flacks: "If your opponent has ever spent 17-large on bocce balls or decided to spontaneously polka in public, whatever you do, don't swim nude with drunken teenagers."

It was October 1990. Grunseth had won the GOP nomination for governor and was giving Perpich a run for his money.

Then a story in the *Minneapolis Star-Tribune* alleged that Grunseth had encouraged four young teenage girls to go skinny-dipping with him at his house almost 10 years earlier. The paper reported that affidavits made by two women who were young teens at the time alleged that beer was served to minors at the party and some of the teens and adults had taken off their swimsuits.

One of the women also said that when one girl, a 13-year-old, resisted Grunseth's invitation, he tried to remove the strap of her swimsuit top.

A woman, who was 14 at the time of the alleged incident and a friend of Grunseth's daughter, said of the antics at the party, "I think that is extremely inappropriate behavior for someone who wants to be governor."

Yeah, it's also extremely inappropriate behavior for someone who wants to water your plants, but then Grunseth wasn't running for governor at the time so it might not have seemed that important.

Initially, Grunseth was defiant, saying the allegations were "political terrorism" and "absolutely false." He said Perpich was the "driving force" behind them and a man who "will do anything to stay in office."

But after the *Star-Tribune* reported that he'd had an adulterous affair in the early '80s, his dreams of removing Little Mermaid bikini tops as Minnesota's 37th governor were finally shattered.

He withdrew from the race.

According to the paper, he'd cheated with a young 20-something of his acquaintance.

"Mr. Grunseth acknowledged to the newspaper that he had had an affair with the woman, Tamara Taylor, now 32, of Minnetonka, but he said it ended 'a long time ago, in the early '80s,'" said an October 1990 *New York Times* report on Grunseth's withdrawal. "He divorced his first wife, Katharine Winston, in 1983, and remarried in 1984.

"Ms. Taylor told the newspaper that she met Mr. Grunseth at a party at his home in 1979, when he was married to his first wife, and that their affair began in 1980 and continued intermittently. She said they last had sex together in July 1989, when she met Mr. Grunseth in Washington."

In a strange twist, Perpich lost the general election to Arne Carlson, who had been Grunseth's Republican primary opponent.

Grunseth had, of course, won the primary after campaigning on conservative and family values. As if you hadn't guessed.

23.

The Porn-Watching, Pubic-Hair-Spotting Clarence

Common Name:
Clarence Thomas

Distinctive Habits:
Porn-watching

Distinctive Mating Call:
Who put this pubic hair on my . . .

The Clarence Thomas/Anita Hill soap opera was a signal event in the history of American jurisprudence—though one that's nevertheless begun to fade through the mists of time.

Indeed, apart from having a vague recollection of unwanted sexual advances the Supreme Court nominee allegedly made toward his subordinate coworker, what most people remember are the weirdly vulgar comments he directed her way.

Sadly, what might have been a valuable civics lesson on the Senate confirmation process would quickly turn into the worst frickin' product placement of all time.

From Anita Hill's October 11, 1991, testimony to the Senate Judiciary Committee:

Hill: Well, I recall specifically that the incident about the Coke can occurred in his office at the EEOC.

Senator Joseph Biden: And what was that incident again?

Hill: The incident with regard to the Coke can that's spelled out in my statement.

Biden: Would you describe it once again for me, please?

Hill: The incident involved his going to his desk, getting up from a work table, going to his desk, looking at this can and saying, "Who put pubic hair on my Coke?"

Of course, it was Thomas's conduct as a Supreme Court justice, more than his salacious locker-room talk, that would ultimately prove most troubling—in particular his vote with a narrow majority to stop the recount process in Florida in 2000 and effectively hand the presidency to George W. Bush (at a time when Thomas' wife was busy collecting resumes at the conservative Heritage Foundation for possible Bush administration staffers). Soon, Americans were asking, "Who put this pubic hair on my electoral process? Who put this pubic hair on my Constitution? By God, who put this pubic hair on my country?"
But Hill wasn't done:

Biden: Are there any other incidences that occurred in his office with just—in his office, period?

Hill: There is—I recall at least one instance in his office at the EEOC where he discussed some pornographic material, or he brought up the substance or the content of pornographic material.

Biden: Again, it's difficult, but for the record, what substance did he bring up in this instance at EEOC in his office? What was the content of what he said?

Hill: This was a reference to an individual who had a very large penis and he used the name that he had been referred to in the pornographic material.

Biden: Do you recall what it was?

Hill: Yes, I do. The name that was referred to was Long Dong Silver.

Cue Strom Thurmond spit take.

It got worse, of course. While lame office humor alone might never have scandalized a nation so thoroughly nourished on a steady diet of ironic detachment, Hill also detailed Thomas's alleged clumsy advances:

> *Hill:* I think the one that was the most embarrassing [incident] was his discussion of pornography involving these women with large breasts and engaged in a variety of sex with different people or animals. That was the thing that embarrassed me the most and made me feel the most humiliated.

> *Biden:* If you can, in his words, not yours, in his words can you tell us what on that occasion he said to you? You have described the essence of the conversation. In order for us to determine—can you tell us in his words what he said?

> *Hill:* I really cannot quote him verbatim. I can remember something like, "You really ought to see these films that I've seen or this material I've seen. This woman has this kind of breasts that measure this size and they've got her in there with all kinds of things. She's doing all kinds of different sex acts," and you know, that kind of—those were the kinds of words, where he expressed his enjoyment of it and seemed to try to encourage me to enjoy that kind of material as well.

> *Biden:* Did he indicate why he thought you should see this material?

> *Hill:* No.

Biden: Why do you think—what was your reaction? Why did you think he was saying these things to you?

Hill: Well, coupled with the pressure about going out with him, I felt that implicit in this discussion about sex was the offer to have sex with him, not just to go out with him. There was never any explicit thing about going out to dinner or going to a particular concert or movie. It was, "We ought to go out," and given these other conversations, I took that to mean, "We ought to have sex, or we ought to look at these pornographic movies together."

Dude, seriously. FTD's got a Web site now. Maybe think about going that route next time, 'k sport?

24.
The Parking Californian

Common Name:
Ken Calvert

Distinctive Behaviors:
Voting for
impeachment;
parking with
prostitutes

Natural Habitat:
California watering
holes

In September of 2006, Citizens for Responsibility and Ethics in Washington named California's Ken Calvert to their list of the "20 Most Corrupt Members of Congress."

According to the organization, "Calvert pushed through an earmark to secure $8 million for an overhaul and expansion of a freeway interchange near property he owned, thereby increasing its value nearly 80 percent."

So we have yet another politician who cynically betrays the public interest in favor of short-term personal gain, seeking to line his own pockets under the guise of serving his constituents.

*Bor-*ing.

Face it, the last thing anyone wants to read about is another sketchy land deal, and the average American understands earmarks about as well as the Einstein-Podolsky-Rosen paradox.

The late '90s was an idyllic period for the GOP, when any idiot with an elephant pin could stand up proud, puff up his chest, and call for the president's head.

"We can forgive the actions. We can't forget what occurred," said Calvert, who would later vote in favor of impeachment.

Oh, but if only people could forget Calvert's past.

You see, long before Bill and Monica's little indiscretion, ol' Ken was caught up in a little sex scandal of his own. The *Washington Post* described that first heady blush of new love like this:

"What happened to California Rep. Ken Calvert two months ago is really what politicians' nightmares are all about. The freshly divorced Republican went out to a bar in Corona, Calif., and met one Lore Lindberg, whom he happily bought a drink and offered to drive home in his rented car. Somewhere along the route, the two parked to talk and were briefly questioned by police at 12:30 A.M. on Nov. 28. She soon split; he drove on."

Sounds innocent enough, right? Two devil-may-care singles out for a little drinkypoo, a little drivey-drive, and a little talky-talk . . . what could be more normal?

Unfortunately, there was more to it. Apparently the local press thought the story reeked like a halibut left in the backseat of a Beetle on a hot summer day in Calcutta, so they decided to do a little further research on Ms. Lindberg.

It turned out Lore was a lady of the evening—and he her gallant lord.

Still, she claimed that she wasn't working that evening and that no sex had occurred between her and Calvert. As explanations go, this ranks right up there with . . . well, there really is nothing to compare it to. This is what philosophers of ethics would refer to as the *summum lamus explanatum*. Face it, when you're caught in a car with a hooker, having a little egg on your face is the best possible outcome. You're obviously gettin' some. You might as well cop to it.

So there was blood in the water, to say the least.

Wrote the *Post:* "His detractors are clamoring for him to speak up, and his supporters insist Calvert didn't know Lindberg was a lady of the night and that the whole situation is nothing more than an embarrassment."

In a statement, Calvert defied his critics, saying, "I should not have to tell people what I didn't do especially when NO ONE has accused me of doing anything improper. I am a 40-year-old, single male and my private life shall remain private."

Oh, that halibut wasn't getting any fresher.

Eventually, the original Corona police report came out, and it couldn't have sounded more, well, prostitutey. Here's what the officer on the scene wrote about the encounter. (It's especially helpful if you hum the *Love Boat* theme while you read this.)

"I observed a male subject in the driver seat. . . . As I made my way to the driver door, a female immediately sat up straight in the front passenger seat. It appeared as if her head was originally laying in the driver's lap. . . . Both subjects were extremely nervous. I noticed that the male subject was placing his penis into his unzipped dress slacks, and was trying to hide it with his untucked dress shirt. . . . [The male subject] started his vehicle and placed it into drive and proceeded to leave. I ordered him three times to turn off the vehicle and he finally stopped and complied. . . .The male identified himself by his California Driver's License as Kenneth Stanton Calvert. . . . Calvert continued to cover his unzipped pants with his hands and stated 'We're just talking that's all, nothing else.' . . .

"I spoke with Lindberg separately. I asked her if she had ever been arrested for anything, and she said, 'Yes, for prostitution and under the influence of heroin.' Lindberg said she last 'shot up' approximately one week prior and is currently on methadone."

Awww. Almost makes you tear up, doesn't it? Sounds a little like the film *Love Story,* actually—if Ali MacGraw were a smack-addict whore and Ryan O'Neal were paying her to go down on him in a car.

Then again, it's only fair to give guys caught in cars with prostitutes the benefit of the doubt. Perhaps the conversation went a little something like this:

> *Calvert:* Today I was able to secure a key funding measure in the House Omnibus Appropriations Bill that will benefit leading alfalfa and sorghum growers in my district.

Lindberg: Hmmm. While I had initially planned simply to exchange an epic, ball-draining blow job for some much-needed capital, I have to admit that is fascinating. Tell me more, as I briefly and with absolutely no sexual overtones rest my head in your lap.

Calvert: You see, the appropriations process is like a series of tubes . . .

Of course, the funniest part may be that Calvert apparently was considering fleeing the scene. Yeah, conducting a high-speed chase with your penis nestled in the jagged teeth of your zipper while a strung-out prostitute sits next to you urging you on is probably not the wisest course for a new congressman.

Interestingly, Calvert's exploits would later make it into *The Flynt Report,* *Hustler* publisher Larry Flynt's exposé on the sex lives of Bill Clinton's critics. Calvert's entry was titled, "Touched by a Hooker."

Calvert would later blame his behavior on a number of personal issues, including his wife leaving him and his father's suicide.

You know, it would be nice if just once a politician 'fessed up and said, "Ya know, I just always wanted to bone a hooker."

Apparently, the voters in his district bought the whole my-dad-killed-himself-so-I-bought-a-blow-job logic. He won reelection by a 17-percent margin.

Maybe they should just go ahead and change it from "the party of family values" to "the family for party values."

25.
The Rocky Mountain Porn-Peddling Larry Jack

Common Name:
Larry Jack Schwarz

Distinctive Behavior:
Allegedly collecting child porn

Unique Skills:
Shipping adult porn

In December of 2001, Colorado State Parole Board member and former Republican state representative Larry Jack Schwarz was fired from his job after a local judge signed a warrant to search for child porn in his home.

Amid allegations of sexual abuse leveled by Schwarz's then-43-year-old stepdaughter, who claimed Schwarz had molested her as a child, authorities seized a cache of assorted pornography, including fifteen comic books that a sheriff's investigator described in a court document as "primarily black-and-white drawings in a coloring-book-style format, many containing full-page depictions of adults having sex with children, children having sex with children, and children having sex with animals."

The woman alleged that Schwarz had begun "training" her at 4 years of age and abused her until she was 18. According to a story in Denver's *Rocky Mountain News*, the stepdaughter alleged that Schwarz "made her watch him have sex with her mother and would ask her 'test questions' the next day to make sure she paid attention."

Okay, so up to this point it basically just sounds like the monthly "Where Are They Now?" column from the Republican National Committee newsletter.

And for some strange reason, charges were never filed. But then Colorado authorities know more about law enforcement than any of us do. After all, they appointed Larry Jack Schwarz to the State Parole Board.

Now, also among Schwarz's stash were photos of 25-year-old Jewel DeNyle, "a stage name for a member of Schwarz's family," according to the *Denver Post*. You'll want to remember that name, as it will become important later in our story.

Fast forward to three years later. A reporter from the *Rocky Mountain News* catches up with Schwarz and writes a feature story on his new post-scandal life.

Was he now a repentant preacher? A crusading, antiporn lobbyist? A deeply penitent private citizen who decided to live his life quietly and humbly outside the glaring spotlight of politics?

Not quite.

The man who had left public life in disgrace over a porn scandal involving disturbing allegations from his stepdaughter had, well, entered the porn business as an employee of one of his other daughters.

Seriously.

That's a little like Bill O'Reilly opening up a tahini and falafel stand in Manhattan with Andrea Mackris's college roommate.

Yes, Larry Jack Schwarz was now working for Platinum X Pictures, a hard-core porn outfit in California. The company was co-owned by one Jewel DeNyle (a.k.a. Stephany), who also starred in the films.

"I feel no shame, as I have learned that what we do in our office is no different than any other business," Schwarz told the *Rocky Mountain News*. "It is the adult-entertainment industry, and it's not violent like what you see in real-life daily news or in mainstream movies."

Okay, Larry? It's a little different. While watching footage from, say, the Iraq insurgency or a local gangland slaying may be grim, Katie Couric is rarely posed in anything more revealing than a bustier and fishnet stockings.

Alas, Larry Jack's role in the family business was decidedly more banal than, say, anal. He managed the warehouse.

"It is not a porn shop, it is a warehouse distribution center, like any other, shipping VHS and DVD products—period," said Schwarz.

Of course, a more accurate description would have been "it is a warehouse distribution center, like any other that ships numerous videos of my daughter exchanging fluids with people she also happens to be 1099ing."

For their part, Schwarz's former political comrades seemed to be taken aback by his new career path.

"I could put my finger in an electrical socket and I wouldn't get this kind of a shock," said Ken Chlouber, a Colorado legislator. "If you knew Larry, none of this fits."

"When you have children, why in the world would you promote them doing pornography?" said Norma Anderson, another legislator.

But his new colleagues were apparently not the blue-nosed scolds his erstwhile associates turned out to be.

"I think it's great that Jewel's parents have an open mind about their daughter being in the adult industry," said Michael Stefano, who was a co-owner of the company as well as a performer, and who costarred with DeNyle in the economically titled *Face Down, Ass Up 2*. "Jewel is very close with both of her parents and would do anything for them."

26.
The Pro-Family Polygamist

Common Name:
Jim Galley

Distinctive Behaviors:
Water treatment;
multiple-marrying

*Distinguishing Char-
acteristics:*
Extreme forgetfulness

In 2006, Republican Jim Galley, a former San Diego water treatment operator, ran for Congress on a "pro-traditional family" platform.

Unfortunately, he forgot to mention it was a traditional fourth-century Bedouin family he was talking about.

In June of 2006, the *San Diego Union-Tribune* did a public records search on Galley and discovered that he "was married to two women at the same time, defaulted on his child support payments and has been accused of abuse by one of his ex-wives."

Galley, who was on his third marriage by the time he ran for Congress, had married his second wife, Beth, in the early '80s when he was still married to his first wife, Terry.

According to the *Union-Tribune,* Galley and Terry were separated for seven months when he married Beth in 1982. However, according to Terry, the papers her attorney had sent to Galley for his signature were never returned. So when news of Galley's second marriage got to Terry, she called to tell him they were still married, and reiterated that she needed him to sign the papers. Galley's divorce from Terry wasn't final until 17 months after he married Beth.

Galley's excuse was that he "honestly thought" his divorce had gone through.

Terry also said she had to go on welfare after separating from Galley and produced court records showing Galley had defaulted on his child support payments in the '80s.

Galley claimed he had only defaulted on payments for several months after injuring his back, but later admitted that his paychecks had been garnisheed for four years (though he claimed that was because of a billing mix-up).

As for the restraining order Beth filed against Galley in 1988 after, according to the *Union-Tribune,* she alleged that he'd "repeatedly punched and kicked her, slapped her son twice and threatened to kill a neighbor," he said the accusations were false, and were made simply to get him out of the house.

As for his political aspirations, Beth was not amused. She went public about her husband's allegedly less-than-family-friendly shenanigans after he ran for office in 2004.

"What galls me the most, one that he has the . . . [nerve] to do this, thinking that he could get away with this and he has for all these years," she said. "[And two] that he's got people believing in him."

Galley lost in a landslide to his primary opponent, Blake Miles, a teacher from El Centro, who, to the best of anyone's knowledge, had never once practiced polygamy.

27.

The Antigay Alleged Gay-Bar-Cruisin' Bauman

Common Name:
Robert Bauman

Native Habitat:
American
Conservative Union

*Distinctive
Characteristics:*
Homosexual tenden-
cies and alcoholism

When Mark Foley was unmasked as a major skeev in the fall of 2006, he attempted to soften the blow to his reputation by blaming liquor.

Now, time was when people were just evil dicks, regardless of how blotto they got in their spare time.

Indeed, it's hard to imagine a guy like, say, Hitler or Pol Pot going on and on about his drinking problem and how much it's spiraled his life out of control. ("Hey Goebbels, check it out. I got totally wasted last night, then me and Mengele and a couple guys from work went to a titty bar, got in our panzers and invaded Poland. Fuck! Step nine is gonna be a bitch!")

Then again, Foley's attempt to find refuge in both alcohol and the easy excuse it provides is hardly new.

In 1980, just as the Reagan Revolution was getting underway, another high-profile Republican congressman got in hot water over his attentions toward boys.

Robert Bauman, the anti-gay rights, anti-ERA, antiabortion, "pro-family" chairman of the American Conservative Union, was charged in Washington, D.C., in early October 1980 with soliciting sex from a 16-year-old, just a month before the historic election that would usher in the age of the Moral Majority.

Bauman soon admitted he had "homosexual tendencies," suffered from alcoholism and had sought counseling for what he called his "twin compulsions," which presumably meant his fondness for both gay sex and alcohol, not actual 16-year-old twins.

Before the scandal hit, Bauman was considered a shoo-in for reelection. But the devout Catholic and married (at the time) father of four soon saw his political ambitions disappear in a poof after saying at a press conference that he would not "deny or confirm the wholesale, numerous reports" alleging he had cruised Washington gay bars in the months prior to the charge. Of course, if you're a congressional representative for a conservative district who has built his career on social conservative values and you can't bring yourself to deny rumors that you've been cruising for gay sex, well, chances are, you're a duck.

Needless to say, Bauman lost his reelection bid.

But at the same press conference where he wouldn't confirm or deny cruising around town looking for hot male-on-male action, Bauman claimed to have turned a corner.

"I have changed," he said. "I am not going back to this grave problem in my life. I have not had a drink since May 1. Ironically, after four months of sobriety, I was confronted with my past conduct."

He also said, "I do not consider myself to be a homosexual. I will not discuss the clinical details. I don't owe it to anyone but my God, and I have confessed to Him and am going forward."

The *Washington Post* later interviewed John F. Harvey, the priest who had counseled Bauman earlier in the year.

According to Harvey, there are plenty of legitimate ways a Catholic can deal with his homosexual feelings other than entering the seminary:

"The process of helping persons involved in homosexuality is hard work that requires setting up for a person what I call an ascetical plan of life," said Harvey.

He later continued: "One of the most important aspects is to help the person develop deep friendships as a means of support. This is his way of expressing his sexuality in a positive way, a form of free sublimation."

And in a final thought that also just happened to be one of the worst-testing card inscriptions in Hallmark's history, Harvey added, "Love does not have to be expressed genitally."

But while reaction from his supporters and constituency was mixed, a few of his old friends stood by him. For instance, Joseph Kesner, who had helped sponsor a roast for the congressman, opted to go the pragmatic route, capturing that circa 1980 Republican zeitgeist beautifully:

"Generally speaking, I abhor homosexuality," Kesner told the *Washington Post*. "What I'm looking at here is a man who said he has a problem and has it under control.

"If he was working with children where he was forming little minds, I might take a different view. . . . But Bob Bauman, whether he's a homosexual or whether he's got four legs, expresses my views in Washington."

Six years later, Bauman recounted his experience in the book *The Gentleman from Maryland,* which is such a perfect double entendre it's hard to believe it was unintentional. The book's subtitle, *The Conscience of a Gay Conservative,* suggested that Bauman had at last accepted his "homosexual tendencies."

"Violent public exposure of my secret life forced me to eventual acceptance of my sexual nature and slowly I am coming to terms with myself," he wrote. "What I seek now is stability, peace, the possibility of mutual love, all goals which for the gay person are difficult in the extreme to obtain. But that is so for almost everyone, isn't it?"

But he also apparently wasn't through trying to deflect blame from himself:

"Obviously, some one person or persons within the Carter administration made a calculated decision to finger me for action."

Seriously, he couldn't have possibly been doing this by accident.

28.

The Mary Jane Catholic Gallagher

Common Name:
Tom Gallagher

Distinguishing Feature:
Divorced and remarried Catholic

Native Habitat:
Florida;
political pasture

How long should an aspiring politician continue to be punished for a divorce that was finalized way back in the '70s?

It all depends. If it was amicable, it's easily forgotten. If the man's wife "sought a restraining order, alleging [he] broke into the marital home after the couple separated, stole the dog, and nearly hit his mother-in-law," that puppy's gonna have the half-life of Uranium-238.

Tom Gallagher found that out in 2006 while running for governor of Florida. As the *St. Petersburg Times* reported, the court file from Gallagher's divorce in 1979 contained both the above bombshell and a tidbit about a long-ago affair involving the Republican hopeful, which took the form of "a deposition given by . . . a 26-year-old legislative aide who was estranged from her husband, in which she acknowledged having an affair with Gallagher starting in 1978."

Gallagher acknowledged fault for the divorce (and also admitted to using marijuana "a long, long time ago"), saying, "I can't say

I'm real proud of my personal life back when I was married. . . .
I do take full responsibility for my actions being the reason for
the divorce." (Gallagher remarried in 1998.)

However, Gallagher, a member of the Roman Catholic Church
(which does not recognize divorce and remarriage), said a rededi-
cation to his faith had transformed him. "Christ does change lives
and I'm a different person because of my relationship with him."

His relationship with Crist was not quite as fulfilling. Gallagher lost the primary election to Charlie Crist, who went on to
win the general election.

29.

The What-Happens-in-Vegas-Stays-in-Vegas Mormon

Common Name:
Jim Gibbons

Native Habitat:
Vegas, baby

Distinctive Behaviors:
Offering a helping
hand . . . possibly
right on your ass

In early October 2006, longtime Republican congressman Jim Gibbons of Nevada was seen as a virtual lock to become the state's next governor.

Then a Vegas cocktail waitress, Chrissy Mazzeo, accused Gibbons, a Mormon, of shoving her against the wall of a parking garage in a clumsy sexual advance after a night of drinking off the Strip.

It quickly became a case of he-said/she-said after that.

He said he was just trying to help her when she appeared to be falling.

And, after initially making a complaint and then withdrawing it, she said she had been pressured and offered money to change her story.

He won the race anyway, and was never charged in the alleged attack.

So while there was smoke, there was no definitive fire.

The burning question, however, was "What was a married congressman and gubernatorial candidate, whose religion prohibits alcohol use, doing out with a Vegas cocktail waitress?"

The whole "Jesus ministered to prostitutes and sinners" excuse won't work here. If Jesus had been running as a Republican for public office in October of 2006, He'd have been scared shitless like everyone else. His opponent would have been running ads day and night about how He'd told George W. Bush to invade Iraq, and that "turn the other cheek" quote would have been plastered all over the airwaves under pictures of guys He'd forgiven who made your average Alabama death row inmate look like the Speaker of the House of Lords. And you can pretty much guarantee one of those apostles would have been outed as a homo. Come on. Philip? (Or FisherOMen212, as he was known in ancient Aramaic chat jargon.)

So the old chestnut about "using bad judgment," which for other politicians covers everything from being stopped for failing to yield at a light to getting caught with a hooker who has an Adam's apple the size of an Igloo cooler, hardly applies when you're running for governor (even in Nevada) as a conservative Republican. (Gibbons was no common conservative, either. In 2005, before the war got more embarrassing than the final two seasons of *Happy Days,* Gibbons said, "tree-hugging, Birkenstock-wearing, hippie, tie-dyed liberals [in Hollywood should] . . . go make their movies and their music and whine somewhere else." He added, "It's just too damn bad we didn't buy them a ticket" to be human shields in Iraq.)

But what lesson did the Lord impart to Gibbons when it came to the whole Mazzeo affair? Don't go out off the Strip with Vegas cocktail waitresses just weeks before a statewide election, you fucking dickhead? Oh no. Christ has a nobler calling for us than that.

"I have to admit that, gosh, I learned an important lesson—never to offer a helping hand to anybody ever again," he said.

30.

America's Not-So-Amicably Divorced Red Rudy

Common Name:
Rudy Giuliani

Also Known as:
America's Mayor

Distinctive Behaviors:
Cross-dressing;
wife-ditching

Divorced Republicans—even twice-divorced Republicans—are certainly no rare breed.

They've got money. They've got power. They've got eager young assistants who have not yet realized that, right around the time they're turning 40, that rich, powerful man they've grown so infatuated with is going to look like one of Ed Gein's lamps and have a prostate the size of Tim Russert's head.

So it was only a matter of time before one of those twice-divorced GOPsters would eventually become a leading candidate for the Republican presidential nomination. And it only made sense that he would be one of the most beloved pols of his day.

Thus, former New York mayor Rudy Giuliani divorcing his second wife, Donna Hanover, in 2002 might have been, under ordinary circumstances, nothing more than a footnote to the 2008 presidential race. Oh, but the devil's in the details.

His very public divorce is certainly not something Giuliani can hide. It was the center ring of a media circus the year after Giuliani became "America's Mayor" in the days following the September 11 attacks on Manhattan's World Trade Center.

And it got ugly.

During the messy ordeal, the public learned:

- Giuliani was openly seeing another woman, Judith Nathan.
- His prostate cancer treatment had for a time made him impotent, and thus unable to officially pound the gavel.
- His announcement at a press conference that he was separating from Hanover caught her by surprise.
- At one point during their marriage, Hanover refused to say if she would vote for her husband for mayor, prompting Giuliani's lawyer, Raoul Felder, to respond, "What kind of wife is that?"
- Hanover was seeking an epic settlement, including hundreds of dollars per month to provide for the family's golden retriever. She ultimately got a multimillion-dollar settlement, the couple's upper East Side co-op, reimbursement of legal fees, child-support payments and, according to Hanover's lawyer, an admission that Giuliani had been "cruel and inhuman." (Though Rudy's lawyers denied the cruel and inhuman bit.)

Oh, he also appeared in drag a few times, but that probably had very little to do with his divorce.

Of course, Giuliani, who married Nathan in 2003, is no doubt well aware that his ex-wife might prove a sticking point when it comes to his presidential aspirations. In the lengthy campaign dossier that was leaked to the press in January 2007, Hanover was listed as one of Rudy's potential "vulnerabilities."

Wrote the *New York Daily News:* "One page cites the explicit concern that he might 'drop out of [the] race' as a consequence of his potentially 'insurmountable' personal and political vulnerabilities.

"On the same page is a list of the candidate's central problems in bullet-point form: his private sector business; disgraced former aide Bernard Kerik; his third wife, Judith Nathan Giuliani; 'social issues,' on which is he is more liberal than most Republicans, and his former wife Donna Hanover."

His relationship with the rest of his family has also apparently been strained. Rudy's son Andrew, best known as the kid who came moments away from getting shot with tranquilizers by NYPD snipers during the mayor's inauguration speech several years back, told the *New York Times* in March of 2007 that he would not campaign with his father, preferring to concentrate on his goal of becoming a professional golfer:

"There's obviously a little problem that exists between me and his wife," he said. "And we're trying to figure that out. But as of right now it's not working as well as we would like."

31.

The Country-Loving Evans-Mate

Common Name:
Craig Schelske

Native Habitat:
Craigslist

Distinctive Behavior:
Republican lovin';
sodomite hatin'

It's odd how country music is often extolled by modern-day conservatives when so much of it is filled to the beams with sex and substance abuse.

Cheatin' husbands, whiskey-drinkin' scoundrels, and all manner of improprieties and indecorous behaviors are tried-and-true staples of the genre.

So is it any surprise when these very qualities are mimicked by both the purveyors and devotees of the art form?

Take the very public divorce of country singer and *Dancing with the Stars* contestant Sara Evans from husband Craig Schelske.

Before Evans filed for divorce, Schelske's social conservative bona fides were as firm as Mark Foley at a spring line launch party for Garanimals. He ran, unsuccessfully, for Congress as a Republican in 2002. He was executive director for the right-wing organization American Destiny, and chairman of Craig PAC, a political action committee that works to elect Republicans nationwide.

He also, according to his wife's court

papers, referred to the costume designer for *Dancing with the Stars* as a "sodomite" and told her how awful it was to have their young children at home when said poof was there.

Hey, short of Yahweh breaking out the pillar-of-salt trick at a Broadway casting call for *Mamma Mia,* it doesn't get much more nipple-engorging for Christian conservatives than that.

But the rest of the story, as recounted in Evans's divorce complaint, puts him a bit outside the conservative mainstream.

Indeed, if it were a country song, it might go a little something like this:

Givin' Back Your Ring

Many times you threatened me and told me I was crazy
You talked a lot and hurt me with your words
You drank and smoked until your head was hazy
Your hateful acts, they made our love absurd
You said you'd take the kids away, my babies
And you wouldn't let them see their mama sing
You frequently watched pornography on each of our three computers, maintained many pornographic photographs, including at least 100 of you posing with your erect penis, and several showing you having sex with other women; plus you maintained "Craigs Lists," many of which involved requests for three-party sex and anal sex, and were composed of personal ads on your personal sex engine involving you and prospective sex partners, (filed herewith as collective Exhibit 1 are nine [9] recent "Craigs Lists" stored in the temporary files on your computers); and treated my gay friend like he had scabies
So that's why I'm givin' back your ring

But if the wording of the complaint (which unavoidably—and unhappily—conjures the image of Schelske and his erect penis standing shoulder-to-shoulder and smiling for photographs, with cigars and Cognacs in their hands, in a smoke-filled back room at the Republican National Convention) weren't embarrassing enough, there's Tom DeLay's peripheral involvement in the whole affair.

Just before the season of *Dancing with the Stars* that featured Evans (and, not coincidentally, liberal talk-show host Jerry Springer) first aired, DeLay sent out a bulk e-mail to drum up support for Evans who, he wrote, "represents good American values in the media."

"We need to send a message to Hollywood and the media that smut has no place on television," said DeLay.

While DeLay's support of Evans may have had something to do with Schelske's support of the Republican Party, the irony didn't end there.

Evans, whose oeuvre includes the songs "Cheatin'" and "True Lies," told the *Chicago Sun-Times* in 2005 that one of her priorities was preventing divorce in America:

"[I]t's the 'promoting family values' that drives Evans, who is married to political consultant Craig Schelske. She performed at the 2004 Republican National Convention, but despite her husband's deep involvement in politics Evans is an entertainer who generally steers clear of political issues when she's in public.

"'I'm not going to step out and be really vocal about anything political,' Evans said. 'I saw what it did to the Dixie Chicks. Now, privately, I definitely have my strong opinions, and I support different groups. My main thing is being an advocate for families, keeping the family unit together, and trying to prevent divorce in America. That's my main platform, and I don't think that could offend anybody.'"

For his part, Schelske who, oh yeah, had also (according to Evans' complaint) banged their nanny, quickly denied the allegations.

He conceded that he sometimes watched adult movies with his wife, and that his wife once took a few nude photos of him—on their tenth anniversary.

He further claimed that Evans filed for divorce a day after he found out she was having an affair, and that her interest in her family flagged after she started on *Dancing with the Stars*.

The he said/she said wrangling would later continue. In February, Evans requested a date for mediation and trial, which prompted a response from Schelske.

"I have insisted that either the proof be produced or that the false allegations be withdrawn or retracted and an apology be issued to begin the process of restoration of my reputation," he said in an affidavit.

"Sara told me she could not figure out a way to retract the allegations and she was 'aghast' at what had been filed. My wife has affirmed privately to me that she was 'mistaken' about the photographs, did not believe them to be photographs of me, and she has stated that she was working on a statement to that extent. As of this date, however, no retraction has been proposed or issued."

In April 2007, the nanny sued Evans for false accusations and Schelske sued one of Evans's lawyers for slander and, as of this writing, it's all just one big clusterfuck.

For updates, you can monitor *Extra* and *Entertainment Tonight*. Or Craigslist. Whichever.

32.
The Ultra-Conservative Idaho Symms

Common Name:
Steve Symms

Distinctive Behavior:
Stage-propping

Native Habitat:
Conservative Idaho

Considered one of the most conservative members of Congress, Senator Steve Symms walked away from a reelection fight in August 1991 under a shroud of controversy.

It wasn't so much what the Idaho Republican did. Lots of guys divorce their wives. But there was some question, at least in his ex's mind, about how he'd conducted himself.

Suffice to say, the Symmses lagged somewhat behind Mark Antony and Cleopatra when it came to history's epic love stories. Hell, they lagged behind Tom Hanks and Wilson the volleyball for that matter.

A June 1991 editorial from the *Times-News* of Twin Falls, Idaho, summed the situation up nicely:

"Fran Symms told a reporter that Symms wooed her into campaigning for him in 1986 by making 'lots of promises' that overcame her doubts about his fidelity.

"Then, after using her as a kind of prop wife to smile beside him on the campaign stump, Symms walked out.

"He duped her, then he dumped her.

"Fran Symms deserves credit for her courage in risking the wrath of her powerful ex-husband and his family to reveal her view of this public figure's private character.

"Her remarks strongly hint that there is truth in the long-circulated rumor of Symms' philandering. More than that, they show a manipulative and coldly mercenary attitude toward an intimate relationship.

"Granted, that's just her side of the story. The senator refuses to tell his side."

You know, Steve, *The Stepford Wives* was just a movie.

Seriously.

33.
The Boozin', Womanizin' Texas J. T.

Common Name:
John Tower

Native Habitat:
Probing Iran-contra

Distinctive Behavior:
Not one to turn
down a drink,
or T and A

Former Texas Senator John Tower is perhaps best known for his role as the head of the Tower Commission, the investigative body that probed the Iran-Contra scandal. But it was a humiliating Senate confirmation fight that would ultimately make him infamous.

In 1989, Tower, who looked a little like Billy Barty on bovine growth hormone, failed in his bid to become George H. W. Bush's secretary of defense.

While the Senate Armed Services Committee might have reasonably rejected his nomination on the grounds that the chief military advisor for the most powerful nation in the history of the world must never be allowed to be photographed sitting on a mushroom, it was the former senator's allegedly libertine ways that would be his undoing.

Hounded by rumors that he was an incorrigible boozer and womanizer, it was testimony from an ex-wife and a fellow conservative that ironically proved most damaging.

He was twice divorced, and his second wife,

Lilla Burt Cummings, had accused Tower during divorce proceedings of "marital misconduct."

Add to that Paul Weyrich, a renowned activist and key player in conservative circles, questioning Tower's "moral character," and Tower's fate was soon sealed.

"Over the course of many years, I have encountered the nominee in a condition, a lack of sobriety, as well as with women to whom he was not married," said Weyrich. "I encountered it enough that it made an impression."

Senate Armed Services Committee chair Sam Nunn also questioned the wisdom of handing the keys of the military to a man whose Breathalyzer readings would have had to be sent in to Sandia National Laboratories.

"I cannot in good conscience vote to put an individual at the top of the chain of command who has a history of excessive drinking such that he would not be selected to command a missile wing, a [Strategic Air Command] bomber squadron or a Trident missile submarine," said Nunn. "Leadership must be established from the top down."

Translation: Hit the bricks, Caligula.

The committee ultimately voted to reject Tower's nomination, which set the stage for a 53–47 defeat in the full Senate.

To illustrate how troubled the Senate was by Tower's reputation, Dick Cheney, who many feel is fouler than Andre the Giant's unitard, was confirmed with a 92–0 vote to the same post a short time later.

34.

The Marriage-Protectin', Spouse-Ditchin' Miller

Common Name:
Jeff Miller

Also Known as:
"The Great
Hypocritus"

Distinctive Behavior:
Protecting marriage,
in theory

There are a lot of flagrant ironies in this world: the North Korean government calling itself the Democratic People's Republic of Korea; the Clear Skies Act of 2003; the McDonald's McDLT, which dedicated so many of our nation's best and brightest minds—and so much of our nation's precious blood and treasure—into finding a way to keep the hot side hot and the cool side cool, while tragically failing to ever really accomplish either.

But as ironies go, they don't get much richer than former Tennessee state senator Jeff Miller, the sponsor of the state's antigay Marriage Protection Act, reaching a divorce settlement in the wake of a rumored affair with a female staffer.

In response to the divorce settlement, Miller said he and his wife, Brigitte, had "amicably resolved all marital differences, and our divorce is final." But in a statement that showed more balls than a Phil Gramm movie, Miller pleaded for privacy, saying he and his ex "have no intentions of publicly commenting further on this issue and are hopeful this will end the inquiries into our private matters."

Tennessee Democratic Party Chairman Bob Tuke noticed the "grotesque, utter hypocrisy" of promoting something called the Marriage Protection Act while engaged "in the middle of a flagrant affair."

Indeed, his wife had claimed in court documents that Miller had been involved in "inappropriate marital conduct," whereas published reports named a former member of his staff as his "girlfriend."

"It sets a terrible example, and our elected officials don't need to be behaving that way," said Tuke. "I hope he is able to put it behind him, but that doesn't change the hypocrisy."

Miller, who for a time was one of the individuals being investigated in a wide-ranging public corruption probe (though he was not among those arrested), later stepped down as the Republican Senate caucus chairman and announced he would not seek reelection.

"Time demands and constraints that the legislature places on elected officials have become enormous for those with families and for those of us who have to make a living in another profession," he said.

Of course, his less-than-forthcoming statement hardly made up for the fact that his failed marriage merely cheapened every loving, faithful, God-ordained, hot male-on-male union in the country. Not to mention that being a kid is hard enough as it is, so why would you ever want to add the confusion of a father who's banging his legislative aide on top of it?

35.
The Blustering Bob

Common Name:
Bob Dornan

Natural Enemies:
"Spear-chucking
lesbians"

Distinctive Behavior:
Tying Democratic
presidents to the
KGB

If ever there was a standard-bearer for conservative lunacy in Congress, it was California's Bob Dornan.

In his book *Rush Limbaugh Is a Big Fat Idiot,* Al Franken described Dornan as a "crazy homophobe." And in 1994, Nathan Callahan and William Payton released *Shut Up, Fag!: Quotations from the Files of Congressman Bob Dornan, the Man Who Would Be President.* The sole customer review for the book at Amazon. com gives it five stars, and says, "I had always suspected he might be nuts, now I know."

The reviewer is not alone.

Indeed, at the press conference announcing his 1996 Republican presidential bid, Dornan seemed to be well aware that his reputation as a complete and utter fucking lunatic had preceded him.

"There are a lot of unfair liberal journalists who are a little bit too much into the '60s and advocacy that have created a mythical Bob Dornan that doesn't exist—someone who beats his grandchildren and who is a mean curmudgeon in the cloakroom," he said.

But while Dornan was doing his best to project mental clarity, by most accounts he behaved the way Gary Busey might if you bought him a subscription to *National Review*. According to an April 1995 *Houston Chronicle* story on his quixotic presidential bid, the former talk-show host, C-SPAN favorite, and sometime Rush Limbaugh fill-in:

- Once referred to an opponent's supporters as "spear-chucking lesbians."
- Once grabbed a Democratic congressman by the collar, calling him a wimp for not serving in Vietnam.
- Attempted to reveal that a fellow Republican House member was gay, without the congressman's permission.
- Called a former Soviet television commentator "a self-betraying little Jew."
- Liked to tell people that his birth date, April 3, 1933, was the same calendar date as Christ's crucifixion.
- Accused President Clinton of aiding the enemy during Vietnam. Without proof, he also claimed on the House floor that Clinton traveled to Moscow as a guest of the KGB as a student and also accused the president of "multiple adulteries."

But some of his colleagues thought he wasn't all that bad. Indeed, Texas congressman Gene Green told the *Chronicle* that Dornan "seems real friendly in the halls and elevators."

Well, that may be, but if you're going to question another man's marital conduct, you better make sure there's nothing in the public record about you pulling a gun on your wife just prior to pouring milk on her head.

According to the *New York Daily News*, "Dornan's wife, Sallie, claimed in four separate divorce actions from 1960 to 1976 that the right-winger had beaten her and subjected her to 'extreme cruelty,' both mental and physical.

"At one point, a restraining order was issued against Dornan. Sallie signed a statement that Dornan had 'pull[ed] her through the house by the hair, producing a revolver and pouring a quart of milk over her head."

After the couple got back together, Sallie claimed it had been a toy gun. "He didn't have any guns then," she explained.

Sallie got another restraining order after filing for divorce for the third time, and Dornan violated it.

Later, Dornan's wife would retract all the allegations. "Every word of every charge and hurtful allegation was totally false," she said, explaining that she had been addicted to sedatives, painkillers, and alcohol. "My lies, even in court, were born of illness and my confusion brought about by those prescription drugs and the sad, self-serving tragic advice of my mother. . . ."

She also disclaimed her allegations of abuse, saying Dornan was "just a big, loud, blustering man."

In 1996, after seeing his presidential aspirations go the way of his mental cohesion, Dornan faced a challenge for his House seat from Democrat Loretta Sanchez.

Before the election, the *OC Weekly* quoted a confident Dornan, who cited his paterfamilias status and military record as sure guarantees of reelection.

"She can't beat me," he said. "Bob Dornan is a father of five, grandfather of 10, military man, been married 41 years. She has no kids, no military, no track record. I win."

He lost.

DIDJAKNOW?

Family-values darling Ronald Reagan was married twice. His first wife, Jane Wyman, with whom he had children, cited "extreme mental cruelty" when divorcing him in 1948.

36.
The Illegally Adulterous Georgian Bowers

Common Name:
Mike Bowers

Distinctive Behaviors:
Selective defense of archaic statutes; adultery

Distincive Calls:
"Did that make me a hypocrite? Yes."

Everyone knows there are laws on the books—often bizarre "blue laws"—that aren't *really* laws anymore.

For instance, according to the Web site dumblaws.com, in Alabama it's illegal to wear a false mustache that causes laughter in church; in Texas it can be a felony to promote the use of or to own more than six dildos; and in South Dakota it's illegal to fall asleep in a cheese factory.

The Bible can be similarly picayune and archaic. For instance, it's forbidden to give any of your children over for sacrifice to Molech which, granted, may have been a big problem once but is hardly burning up the phone lines at Interpol these days.

It's also forbidden to cook a young goat in its mother's milk (the actual tenth commandment—see Exodus 34: 26–28), and if you're a dwarf or a Moabite or have crushed testicles or bad eyesight or, God forbid, are a Moabite dwarf with crushed testicles and an astigmatism, you're not allowed in church.

So with all that ample spiritual baggage

being carried around these days, it's fair to ask why modern Christians aren't going apeshit over Dipsy, the stunted Teletubby with the unspeakably mangled gonads.

And why aren't Christians protesting at the funerals of people who died from accidentally walking into open sewers?

Why the almost monomaniacal focus on gays? (Indeed, if anything, these other ancient laws pose an even bigger problem for modern, compassion-minded Christians, as "hate the crushed testicles, love the crushed-testicles-guy" doesn't really work on any level.)

Whatever the reason, it's become painfully clear that when it's time to defend a law everyone knows is bullshit and antithetical to the values of a contemporary liberal democracy, the edict that's generally chosen as a bulwark against the ravaging tides of modernity is not the one about dozing amid creaking pallets of ripe Gorgonzola but the one having to do with where certain men like to put their wee-wees.

And so it came to pass that in 1986 Georgia attorney general Mike Bowers took up the cudgel on behalf of every decent Southern patriot, arguing before the United States Supreme Court in defense of the state's antisodomy law.

It all started when Michael Hardwick, a big ol' gay, was arrested by Atlanta police in 1982 for having sex with another man. Though prosecutors decided against pursuing the case, Hardwick sued to test the Georgia law.

The statute was successfully defended by Bowers. (Eventually, Georgia's antisodomy law was invalidated by the Georgia Supreme Court, and later all such laws were struck down in the United States in 2003's Supreme Court case *Lawrence v. Texas*.)

While some might argue he was simply faithfully executing his office on behalf of the state of Georgia, Bowers had also angered gay-rights activists with a series of other actions. For instance, he had ruled that college newspapers could not refuse antigay ads, and that the city of Atlanta couldn't include domestic partners in its benefits packages. He also withdrew a job offer from a lesbian who had planned on marrying a woman, claiming the marriage would violate the state's antisodomy laws.

So with this level of scrupulousness in his public life, there simply had to be a mistress hiding somewhere, if not an armoire full of hot nipple clamps and simultaneous common-law marriages to three of the five founding members of Menudo.

Well, sometimes our dreams only come half true.

In June of 1997, Bowers admitted he'd had a more than decade-long affair with, alas, a woman while serving as Georgia's attorney general.

The admission came shortly after he'd resigned as AG to launch his campaign for governor.

At the time, Bowers had been married to his wife for 33 years and, according to the AP, said they had separated for several years during the affair but had gotten back together. Bowers said the other woman was a former employee.

Naturally, this violated any number of written and unwritten laws, including a Georgia law that was still on the books forbidding adultery.

Reaction to the news was mixed. Robin Shahar, the lesbian he'd decided not to hire, quickly pointed out the hypocrisy.

"When he stands up in federal court and makes the argument he's making about sodomy while knowing that people in his own office—including himself—are committing adultery, it's very troubling."

To be fair, Bowers gutted it up and admitted he had been less than consistent. When asked if withdrawing Shahar's job offer while he was nailing a woman not his wife was hypocritical, Bowers said, "In a moral sense, yes. But legally, I do not believe there was any . . . [alternative]. Did that make me a hypocrite? Yes."

Of course, the forgiveness that flows like milk and honey for wayward Republicans and mysteriously turns to ash in the mouths of Democrats was in abundant supply once again.

Said Jerry Keen, the then president of the Christian Coalition in Georgia: "It's disappointing when our leaders make these type of mistakes. . . . Once all the details come out, I would not deny that there are going to be some people for whom this is going to be a major issue. . . . For others, they're going to say he admitted this and let's move on. One of the real tenets of Christianity is forgiveness."

Less than a year later, *George* magazine interviewed Anne Davis, who claimed she was the woman with whom Bowers had conducted his lengthy affair.

According to the story, Davis, Bowers' former secretary and an ex–Playboy Club waitress, said she dated Bowers for fifteen years, and had taken a romantic trip with him just six weeks before he announced his bid for governor. Perhaps most damaging, Davis claimed Bowers was still sending her money to help with household expenses.

The Bowers campaign tried to spin the interview as best they could, essentially arguing that it was of little consequence for a candidate who, metaphorically speaking, had already been buggered silly.

"We're not going to get in the business of reacting to this story," spokesman Bill Crane told reporters. "Mike's been candid, honest and voluntary in all the disclosures made to date. The public knows more about Mike's marriage, private life and failings than perhaps any candidate in the history of the state. They'll have to weigh this information against what he's honestly disclosed."

For the record, Mike Bowers is not now nor has he ever been governor of the state of Georgia.

37.
The Big-House-Headed Speaker

Common Name:
Edison Misla
Aldorando

Native Habitat:
Puerto Rico

Distinctive Behavior:
Trying to get girls
to go wild

There's a stubborn myth that all Republican politicians are white, privileged Anglo-Saxons sucking at the corporate teat with the sort of reckless vigor that could only come from a heritable sense of entitlement handed down from European feudalism and the legally impervious landowning aristocracy of pre-Civil War America.

But the RNC is doing a lot to expand its base and, when it comes to scandals, they're all about affirmative action.

Edison Misla Aldarondo was the Republican speaker for Puerto Rico's House until he resigned after being indicted on corruption charges.

Now, most people fresh off an indictment know it's probably best to lie low for a little while. If you're arrested for DUI, you don't go into Fantastic Sam's waving Nick Nolte's mug shot, suck down a case of Hamm's and a bottle of tequila, and drive your drug-mule buddies to the Tijuana border in a red convertible tricked out with a backseat pony keg and a "Bad Cop, No Doughnut" bumper sticker.

But Aldarondo apparently didn't have the epiphany that normally goes with such chastening experiences. Instead, he decided to focus his energies at home.

In the summer of 2002, while a 17-year-old friend of his stepdaughter visited their house, the former speaker decided to liven the evening by serving the girls alcohol. He followed this up with an assault on the friend.

He was eventually convicted of intoxicating the two girls and attempting to rape the friend, and was sentenced to 13 years in prison. He was also sentenced to 10 years following a separate conviction for fondling his stepdaughter.

Who knows, when he gets out of prison perhaps he'll celebrate by illegally downloading some movies, kicking a homeless person, shivving a Carmelite nun, and setting up a fake money-order scam through his phony Nigerian bank account.

38.
The Breaking-and-Entering Colorado Dougie

Common Name:
Doug Dean

Habitat:
Colorado (also
spotted in basement
and bedroom of
ex-girlfriend)

Distinctive Call:
"I do acknowledge I
used poor judgment"

If there's a modern-day companion to the classic dictum "hell hath no fury like a woman scorned," it's no doubt "hell hath no fury like a Colorado House speaker who uses a screwdriver to break into the home of his ex-girlfriend, Gloria Sanak, and then sits in her darkened bedroom like Hannibal Lecter's less charismatic cousin until she comes home and calls 911 in a desperate, bloodcurdling panic."

According to the *Denver Post*, on May 9, 2001, Sanak broke up with Colorado House speaker Doug Dean over the phone. Then, sometime after midnight, Dean arrived at the house the two had been sharing for several months, found some of his clothes outside the house, and, after discovering the locks had been changed, parked a block away, returned to the house, scaled a fence, and jimmied open a basement window.

When she returned home, she found him there. They had a short talk, she ran to the home of a police sergeant she knew as Dean followed, and then Dean spoke with the sergeant and waited while Sanak called 911 and police arrived.

Okay, so far it doesn't sound too terribly tawdry. Indeed, if eHarmony.com were taking out full-page ads targeting prominent GOP legislators, this is probably about the best testimonial they could come up with.

But then the media got hold of the 911 tape and it wasn't so cute anymore.

Sanak's 911 call, which TheDenverChannel.com—the Web site of Denver's ABC affiliate—described as "frantic," was released to the media in response to a *Rocky Mountain News* public records request.

Wrote TheDenverChannel.com: "The out-of-breath Sanak told the dispatcher that 'I had kicked out my boyfriend and he broke in one of the windows and he was waiting in the house when I got there.' . . . Sanak was crying and appeared to be gasping for breath as she urged the dispatcher to send help immediately. The sound of terror in her voice is unmistakable, according to the *News*. When the dispatcher asked Sanak if Dean was still there, Sanak yelled back. 'Yes, yes,' she said."

Sanak requested a restraining order, but a judge soon removed it at Sanak's request, and Dean was never arrested or charged with a crime because, as the *Denver Post* reported, the district attorney said Sanak had consistently said she didn't think Dean was violent or had trespassed.

Still, some domestic violence groups were troubled by the lack of action against Dean, and believed he should have been arrested under the state's mandatory arrest law.

Said Diana Protopapa of Colorado Coalition Against Domestic Violence, "We still strongly believe that if Doug Dean did break in to coerce or to control, that is domestic violence."

As for Dean, he eventually showed he had at least as much facility for stating the obvious as for breaking and entering:

"I do acknowledge I used poor judgment," he said in a statement. "Believe me, if I had to do it over again, I would not have entered the house that night."

39.
The Lobbyist-Loving Lawmaker

Common Name:
Stephen LaTourette

Mating Habitats:
Diddling the lobbyist

Mating Ritual:
Getting rid
of the old spouse
over the phone

A congressman divorcing his wife and marrying a younger woman is hardly big news. It's a little like reporting that a fan got drunk at a NASCAR event and sustained minor injuries.

The same congressman marrying a lobbyist—his former chief of staff—who has conducted business in front of a committee where he's a ranking member?

Better. Maybe like reporting that a NASCAR fan got drunk, sustained injuries, and, when searched, was found with a firearm, a nineteenth-century whalebone corset, and a signed, dog-eared copy of the official Hanson biography.

However, what really put the case of Ohio Republican Steve LaTourette over the top was the reaction of his ex to, well, him.

Chances are, the former Mr. and Mrs. LaTourette skipped the whole obligatory "let's stay friends" speech.

In a 2003 interview, LaTourette's ex-wife, Susan, told Washington's *The Hill* that LaTourette had informed her over the telephone that he was dating a female lobbyist and wanted a divorce.

"I think Washington corrupts people," she said. "All they care about is getting reelected. I hate them all."

Then, during LaTourette's 2004 reelection campaign against Democrat Capri Cafaro, Susan put a Cafaro sign up in her yard.

"My congressperson should be honest, truthful and decent, and she best exemplifies those qualities," she told the AP.

Despite his ex's best efforts, LaTourette easily defeated Cafaro. Four months later he was married to Jennifer Laptook, his former chief of staff and a vice president of Van Scoyoc Associates, a Washington lobbying firm.

40.
The Girl-Grabbing Christian Crane

Common Name:
Dan Crane

Distinctive Behavior:
Apologizing a lot;
accepting forgiveness

Habits:
Illinois churches;
at least one
17-year-old page

Ah, the classics.

In 1983, the House of Representatives censured Republican Congressman Dan Crane of Illinois, along with Democrat Gerry Studds, for sleeping with 17-year-old female and male pages, respectively.

Crane had admitted to having sex with the girl several times in 1980.

Naturally, the devout Christian and married father of six immediately stepped up to wash away his sins in the blood of the Lamb—which, frankly, has got to be looking a little like KSM's bathwater by this point.

"We pay for our sins in life, and in making my peace I take comfort that our Lord promised me forgiveness seventy times seven," said Crane. "Regardless of the action this body takes, I want the members to know that I am sorry and that I apologize to one and all."

Knowing that Crane thought he could nail somewhere in the neighborhood of five hundred more teenagers before God so much as sent him a memo is perhaps not encouraging, but love and forgiveness echoed throughout the chamber. Indeed, Henry Hyde, who would later be cast as Pitchfork Wielder #2 in the Monica Lewinsky saga (and who would ultimately have his own indiscretion exposed to the public), pleaded for leniency:

"He is embarrassed, he is humiliated, he is disgraced. And it endures, it is not over," said Hyde. "Every shred of dignity will be stripped away from Dan Crane, and it will endure."

"I suggest to the members that compassion and justice are not antithetical; they are complementary. The Judeo-Christian tradition says hate the sin and love the sinner. We are on record as hating the sin, some more ostentatiously than others. I think it is time to love the sinner."

Just days before his abject mea culpa, however, Crane had seemed a bit more feisty. The man who favored public school prayer, had presented himself as a pious family man, and who had derided the libertine "Washington set" admitted that he had "made a mistake," but was careful to point out that "in no way did I violate my oath of office."

Yes, the congressional oath of office, which begins "I do solemnly swear that I will support and defend the Constitution of the United States against all enemies, foreign and domestic," does not in fact include anything about keeping your love mutton out of high school girls. When oh when will Congress close that glaring loophole?

Crane was defeated in his 1984 reelection bid and returned to dentistry, where they merely make you promise not to grope your patients.

41. The Whitewater Stalker

Common Name:
Robert Ray

Distinctive Characteristics:
Investigating the Clintons

Mating Technique:
Alleged stalking

Sometimes you wonder if there isn't some weird curse surrounding the Monica Lewinsky affair—like it's the King Tut's tomb of political scandals or something.

Witness Robert Ray.

Ray is best known as the independent counsel who in 1999 took over the lengthy multimillion-dollar national colonoscopy that was the Clinton Whitewater investigation.

Of course, in a move that made about as much sense as turning Fonzie into a high school teacher who works with Ted McGinley, the irrepressible Ken Starr would eventually alchemize the Whitewater case into the infamous Monica Lewinsky affair. That's when its ratings really took off.

But at best, Ray himself was doing mop-up duty. The Whitewater/Lewinsky scandal jumped the shark once and for all in early '99 when Clinton was acquitted of impeachment charges, and Starr was smart to get out.

Oh, but the curse lived on.

Fast-forward to May of 2006. Ray was charged with fourth-degree stalking and received a desk-appearance ticket.

The girl in question was Tracy Loughlin, a Manhattanite who worked in magazine promotions.

According to the *New York Post,* "A law-enforcement official said Loughlin . . . ended the relationship with Ray, 46, four months ago but that he has persisted in calling her, sending her e-mails and turning up at places where he figured she might be."

But the *New York Daily News* saw fit to pile on. It reported that, according to his estranged wife's sister, Ray was still married when the alleged stalking occurred.

"My sister has suffered tremendously in the last year and divorce proceedings are well underway," Sarah Lawley, the sister of Ray's wife, Kristen, said. "But they are not divorced yet. . . . This is just another thing that will hurt my sister."

Ray, whom the *Daily News* described as "an outspoken critic of the Clintons," also launched a bid for a New Jersey Senate seat as a Republican before dropping his campaign after just a few weeks.

Hypocrites in the House: The Sordid Sex Lives of the Clinton Witch Hunters

In September of 1998, the U.S. government posted the infamous Starr Report, the lengthiest, costliest, most legally intricate *Penthouse Forum* letter in American history, on the Internet.

It was a watershed moment for representative democracy, the rule of law, the emerging information technology revolution, and the Kimberly-Clark Corporation, manufacturers of Kleenex Facial Tissue With Lotion.

Impeachment fervor was just heating up, and the report would stoke the fires of the nation's outrage and loins, helping to pave the way for President Clinton's attempted ouster.

But there was trouble brewing for the opposing side. Turns out that among the president's loudest critics was a coterie of bounders that had collectively handled more teat than Land O'Lakes.

Indeed, less than a week after the Starr Report tingled the nethers of a great nation, leading Republicans were freaking out over a series of public outings that had started with Representatives Dan Burton and Helen Chenoweth, had just recently embarrassed House Judiciary Committee chair Henry Hyde, and showed few signs of stopping.

Their response, which basically amounted to "hey, knock off this sexual witch-hunt stuff; we thought of it first," may have constituted the single greatest leap forward in human comedy since *Australopithecus afarensis* discovered the spit take during the violent goring of an uncommonly sanctimonious alpha male in circa 3 million B.C.E.

In a letter to Louis Freeh, House Republican leaders asked the FBI director to look into the possibility that people connected with the White House might have been behind the reports—which, let's face it, amounted to the trademark infringement of a popular brand the GOP had struggled for months to establish.

"We are deeply troubled by recent media reports indicating that certain individuals may be engaged in a systematic attempt to intimidate Judiciary Committee Chairman Henry Hyde and other elected members of the House from doing their constitutional duty, by promoting prurient allegations about their personal lives to the media," said the letter which, significantly it would turn out, was signed by then-Speaker Newt Gingrich and seven other Republican leaders.

NEWT GINGRICH

First things first. In March of 2007, in a now-notorious interview with Focus on the Family pooh-bah James Dobson, Gingrich admitted he'd been banging a broad unanointed by God while still married to the bird he married just months after divorcing his first wife, Jackie, who had been his childhood sweetheart (which sounds really cute and wholesome and everything until you realize it would actually be slightly more accurate if you replaced "childhood" with "high school" and "sweetheart" with "geometry teacher").

Jackie was also the woman whom, according to her version of events, Gingrich famously discussed divorce terms with while she was in the hospital recovering from cancer surgery.

"There are times that I have fallen short of my own standards. There's certainly times when I've fallen short of God's standards," a chastened Gingrich said of the affair. (Though it's a safe bet that if God parted the skies and told him he had to go back to nailing his high school geometry teacher, he'd find a way around it.)

"There were times when I was praying and when I felt I was doing things that were wrong. But I was still doing them," he added. "I look back on those as periods of weakness and periods that I'm . . . not proud of."

Significantly, during the period when Newt was having his own little passion on the mount, he was also leading the coup against Clinton. Still, he was able to draw what he interpreted as a meaningful distinction:

"The president of the United States got in trouble for committing a felony in front of a sitting federal judge," he said of the Clinton impeachment. "I drew a line in my mind that said, 'Even though I run the risk of being deeply embarrassed, and even though at a purely personal level I am not rendering judgment on another human being, as a leader of the government trying to uphold the rule of law, I have no choice except to move forward and say that you cannot accept . . . perjury in your highest officials.'"

Of course, while Clinton's actions were certainly worthy of censure, it might have been interesting to see how Gingrich would have reacted to the same sort of full-court press Clinton endured, particularly since he's often been credited with inventing the very same sleazy loophole that's normally attributed to Clinton.

In an August 1998 Salon.com piece, writer Stephen Talbot recalled a *Vanity Fair* article from three years earlier that had neatly pierced Newt's pretensions:

"For one thing, Gingrich pioneered a denial of adultery that some observers would later christen 'the Newt Defense': Oral sex doesn't count. In a revealing psychological portrait of the 'inner' Gingrich that appeared in *Vanity Fair* (September 1995), Gail Sheehy uncovered a woman, Anne Manning, who had an affair in Washington in 1977 with a married Gingrich.

"'We had oral sex,' Manning revealed. 'He prefers that modus operandi because then he can say, 'I never slept with her.' She added that Gingrich threatened her: 'If you ever tell anybody about this, I'll say you're lying.'

"Manning was then married to a professor at West Georgia, the backwater college where Gingrich taught. 'I don't claim to be an angel,' she told Sheehy, but 'he's morally dishonest.'"

In 1980, while Newt was divorcing his first wife, Jackie, she claimed that he had "failed and refused to voluntarily provide reasonable support for herself and their children."

Ironically, throughout his career, Gingrich has passed on few opportunities to paint Democrats as degenerates and moral cripples.

He has at various times referred to them as "traitors," the party of "total bizarreness, total weirdness" and all but blamed them for the deaths of notorious child murderer Susan Smith's two kids.

In 1992, during the Democratic National Convention, he also pontificated on Hollywood and its famously loose morals: "Woody Allen having nonincest with a nondaughter to whom he was a nonfather because they were a nonfamily fits the Democratic platform perfectly."

How that compares with nonsupport for a nonwell first wife whom he cheated on by having nonsex with a nonsingle woman of his former acquaintance is anyone's guess. Let's just call it a horse apiece.

HENRY HYDE

In September 1998, *Salon* reported that Illinois Republican Henry Hyde, the head of the House Judiciary Committee, which gave the green light to the Clinton impeachment, had carried on an adulterous five-year affair thirty years earlier with another man's wife.

It all might have been a little like the scandalous '60s comedy *Bob & Carol & Ted & Alice* if Carol and Ted hadn't realized they were in the movie.

In an interview, the cuckolded Fred Snodgrass spoke of the affair between his ex-wife Cherie and Hyde, who was elected for the first time to the Illinois House while the affair was ongoing. (At the time Hyde was also married with four children.)

"I watched [Hyde] on TV the other night," Snodgrass told Salon. "These politicians were going on about how he should have been on the Supreme Court, what a great man he is, how we're lucky to have him in Congress in charge of the impeachment case. And all I can think of is here is this man, this hypocrite who broke up my family."

Hyde released his own statement to *Salon* shortly before the story ran:

> "The statute of limitations has long since passed on my youthful indiscretions. Suffice it to say Cherie Snodgrass and I were good friends a long, long time ago. After Mr. Snodgrass confronted my wife, the friendship ended and my marriage remained intact. The only purpose for this being dredged up now is an obvious attempt to intimidate me and it won't work. I intend to fulfill my constitutional duty and deal judiciously with the serious felony allegations presented to Congress in the Starr report."

Of course, Hyde neglected to mention that she was a "good friend" he'd set up with her own apartment. One day, after discovering Cherie had her own separate digs, Fred Snodgrass went to see her.

"I'm trying to get in the door, I can see her buttoning up her blouse," said Snodgrass. "And some guy is holding the door, pushing back. It was Hyde. And he's a big guy, I couldn't get in. My wife said she used to tell him, 'What are you doing, trying to hit 300? . . . She stayed in that apartment for a couple years. Every time I went back I'd see new clothes, new furniture—he was keeping her."

While standing in the entranceway of your freshly fertilized mistress's illicit apartment while her husband, who can't get in the door because you're almost comically obese, desperately tries to talk to her is not specifically addressed in the Constitution, it really doesn't sound good—particularly if you're planning on one day being a major player in Operation Let That Be Your Last Blow Job.

DAN BURTON

While he was actually talking about fund-raising activities at the time, Indiana congressman Dan Burton, a family values candidate who used the campaign slogan "character *does* matter," left no doubt what he thought about Bill Clinton in March 1998 interview with the *Indianapolis Star*.

"If I could prove 10 percent of what I believe happened, he'd be gone," Burton told the newspaper. "This guy's a scumbag. That's why I'm after him."

Just a few months later, Burton was fighting his own character issues. Convinced that *Vanity Fair* was poised to out him as a scumbag in his own right, Burton revealed that he'd had his own adulterous affair for which there was incontrovertible DNA evidence. Except *his* telltale stain inconveniently took the form of an illegitimate son to whom he'd sent support payments.

At the same time that the scum was hitting the fan in his personal life, Burton alluded to "friends of the president" who may have been floating rumors.

But it was the "scumbag" comment that prompted Harrison Ullmann, editor of the alternative weekly *NUVO,* to write an unflattering column that helped blow the lid off Burton's past earlier that year. Harrison would later talk to *Salon* about the congressman, assuring the online publication that he "had no contact with the White House or any friends of Clinton's."

In fact, said Ullmann, Burton's escapades had long been legendary among both politicians and journalists.

"In terms of sex, the first place the '60s got to in Indianapolis was the Statehouse—this was a time when hookers would come in and leave cards on legislators' desks," said Ullmann. "Getting a piece was rampant in the General Assembly then. And within that context, Burton had a major reputation."

Ullmann apparently knew Burton so well that he once set up a prank with some lobbyists and lawmakers premised on Burton's libidinous rep.

"There was this night we knew it would be impossible for him to get away, and we told him we were putting together this party and some really great women would be there. He was going nuts, trying to get out of whatever he was locked into."

Indeed, offered Ullmann, Burton's sexual appetites were at least as prodigious as Clinton's.

"Back when he had a seat in the General Assembly and back during his early terms in Congress, Dan Burton had a reputation for sex with convenient women that was at least as awful and awesome as the Clinton reputation," he wrote. "When Hoosier politicians and pundits gathered, they would tell each other stories about Burton scoring with interns and pages, scoring with staffers in his offices and staffers in his campaign, scoring with Carmel housewives and some fine and famous Christian women elsewhere in his district."

HELEN CHENOWETH

About a week after Dan Burton spilled his guts about his carelessly spilled seed, Idaho congresswoman Helen Chenoweth stepped up to the confessional.

The Idaho Statesman outed Chenoweth after she had demanded Clinton resign and had tried to assume the moral high ground in a campaign ad, saying, "I believe that personal conduct and integrity does matter."

In a statement to the newspaper after it had revealed her affair with a married man, she took a slightly different tone. This time, instead of coming off as a supercilious scold, she projected the air of, say, the archangel Gabriel.

"Fourteen years ago, when I was a private citizen and a single woman, I was involved in a relationship that I came to regret, that I'm not proud of," said Chenoweth. "I've asked for God's forgiveness, and I've received it."

Chenoweth also attempted to draw a distinction between herself and the president:

"Since being elected to public office, I have lived my personal life uprightly, in a disciplined way which is worthy of the office entrusted to me," she said.

Considered a far-right conservative (she was dubbed by critics the "poster girl for the militia movement" for her defense of the controversial groups and was also known to hold "endangered salmon bake" fundraisers), she survived the fallout of the scandal and remained a House member through 2000.

But it was a 1996 challenge for her seat that betrayed her true vulnerability. In an October story on the upcoming congressional election, Portland's *Oregonian* reported that "the May primary showed a measure of discontent when a mentally ill man named William Levinger ran against Chenoweth and received 32 percent of the vote only a couple weeks after he went berserk during a Boise TV station interview. Levinger offered a reporter $5,000 for a kiss and proceeded to disrobe until law enforcement authorities carried him away."

God eventually called Helen home, presumably to explain the bit about His forgiving her, in October 2006 after her car flipped on a Nevada highway.

Her Associated Press obit made no mention of the affair, but did note that she had "said that salmon aren't endangered but white males are, complained about black government helicopters harassing ranchers, said minorities didn't like northern Idaho because it is too cold and called for disarming federal resource enforcement agents."

BOB LIVINGSTON

In December of 1998, Texas congressman Tom DeLay, referring to his colleague Bob Livingston's decision to resign from the House, said, " . . . he understood what this debate was all about. It was about honor and decency and integrity and the truth, everything that we honor in this country. It was also a debate about relativism versus absolute truth."

The distinction DeLay had implicitly drawn between Bill Clinton and Livingston, who was poised to lead the party of absolute truth into the twenty-first century as speaker of the House, was clear.

If you get caught in an affair after a concerted rightwing effort to derail your presidency and you resolutely fight to hold onto your office, you're a relativist.

If you resign because the guy who pioneered the full-on beaver shot outsmarted you, you believe in absolute truth.

Indeed, absolute truth descended on House Speaker–designate

Bob Livingston like a dove one crisp winter morn amid reports that Larry Flynt's *Hustler* magazine was set to publish details of his affairs.

Just two days after admitting to marital infidelity, Livingston stood on the floor of the House and challenged the president in no uncertain terms:

"Sir, you have done great damage to this nation over this past year. . . . Say that you have the power to terminate that damage and heal the wounds that you have created. You, sir, may resign your post."

Livingston then shocked House members by actually practicing what he preached.

"And I can only challenge you in such fashion if I am willing to heed my own words," continued Livingston. "I was prepared to lead our narrow majority as speaker, and I believe I had it in me to do a fine job. . . . But I cannot do that job or be the kind of leader that I would like to be under current circumstances. So I must set the example that I hope President Clinton will follow. I will not stand for speaker of the House on Jan. 6."

But in confessing his philandering two days earlier, Livingston sounded a familiar refrain: His sins were not as bad as Clinton's. His "indiscretions were not with employees on my staff, and I have never been asked to testify under oath about them," said Livingston.

For his part, DeLay seemed heartbroken that anyone would stoop so low as to dredge up a man's sexual peccadilloes for political gain:

> "For some, it's no longer good enough to make a mistake, confess that mistake, and accept the consequences of that mistake, and change the way you live your life and keep moving and make a contribution to this country. And I think you ought to think about that—both sides," he said.

This remark was eerily similar to comments he had made to reporters earlier that year.

"When you have a president who in my opinion has cheated on his wife he will cheat on the American people," DeLay said.

Luckily we all know what a moral absolutist DeLay is, or that might come off as just a touch hypocritical.

Bob Barr

Atlanta Journal-Constitution columnist Cynthia Tucker once wrote: "Of Clinton's GOP attackers, [Bob] Barr was the most vociferous, the most overwrought, indeed, the most unhinged."

She might have also added "most likely to lick whipped cream off the bosom of a woman at a Leukemia Society fundraiser" and "most likely to show up as a speaker for the white supremacist Council of Conservative Citizens."

To be fair, Barr appears to have blundered into the CoCC meeting, as his 1999 letter to the editor of *Time* made clear: "The racial views of the C.C.C. are repugnant to me, and I would never have spoken to the group had I known beforehand of its stand," wrote Barr. "It is absurd and irresponsible for anyone to suggest that one speech—during which I discussed only the impeachment process, as I was asked to do—implies that I in any way share or support the group's view." Whether he realized he was licking whipped cream off an actual pair of breasts, as numerous published reports have alleged, is another story, but you're encouraged to check it out for yourself. Granted, information on this sort of thing tends to be sketchy—as of this writing, a Google search of "Bob Barr," "whipped cream" and "ewww" yields just three hits.

More importantly, though, Barr, who arguably had a bigger hard-on for Clinton than for either of his two ex-wives, has hardly been a paragon of virtue.

The man who once said during a House debate on gay marriage, "the flames of hedonism, the flames of narcissism, the flames of self-centered morality are licking at the very foundations of our society" has been married three times, and at least one of his exes said he'd cheated on her. (As Tucker wrote, "Asked about that allegation under oath in a divorce proceeding, he refused to answer. An arcane Georgia law allows individuals to avoid answering questions about adultery if the answers might 'subject them . . . to ridicule or their estates to forfeiture.'")

There's more. For instance, Larry Flynt also made an appearance in the Barr soap opera. Barr was one of 13 House prosecutors during the trial phase of the impeachment, and prior to the trial Flynt produced an unflattering affidavit from Barr's second wife.

It would be unseemly to go into all the details, but suffice to say the allegations had something to do with either an abortion or Rip Taylor's Guatemalan houseboy and a case of almond butter.

Incidentally, of the six House members listed above, each voted yes on all four articles of impeachment against President Clinton, scoring a perfect 24 for 24.

DIDJAKNOW?

Former House Majority Leader Dick Armey, a harsh critic of President Clinton, was accused by at least three women of "inappropriate behavior" while he was a professor at the University of North Texas, according to 1995 profile in the weekly alternative *Dallas Observer*.

Section II
Religiousia Devianti

The rise of the evangelical movement has ushered in a newfound religious conservatism in the United States Selective interpretations of scriptures have given many religious leaders the bludgeon of God-given moral superiority to use on anyone deemed a "sinner" or a fan of *Queer Eye*.

Yet it seems that some of these same people have monopolized perversion in a way that would be unheard of outside of a Caligula-run daycare. And while most atheists have evolved to understand that as an adult you're not supposed to make out with children, the occasional religious leader seems to have missed that particular Bible passage.

So we take a look at these titans of temperance and giants of genuflection, and reveal how it might be safer just to load up your third-graders with strings of beads and send them straight to Mardi Gras.

1.

The Allegedly Kid-Kissin' Florida Baptist

Common Name:
Robert Gray

Distinctive Call:
Condemning the
evils of Elvis

Distinctive Behavior:
Alleged inappro-
priate smooching

On a hot August day in 1956, Pastor Robert Gray stood up and declared that one man had achieved "a new low in spiritual degeneracy" and that "if he were offered his salvation tonight, he would probably say, 'No thanks, I'm on the top.'"

Yes, Gray saw with unjaundiced eyes the future of moral decay and was determined to shine the cleansing light of Christ upon it.

Those gyrating hips. That whiplash smile. That smoldering, penetrating stare that drew impressionable kids, teens, and wobbly-kneed hausfraus inexorably and irretrievably toward the pulsing loins of The Beast.

That's right, kids. He was talking about Elvis.

And though Gray's searing admonitions would do little to tarnish the legacy of the King, they did plenty to boost his fame as a spokesman for the King of Kings. Indeed, his crusade would eventually be celebrated in a classic *Life* magazine photo, with Gray standing next to his pulpit in a smart dark suit and jet-black hair, with a Bible open in his left hand and an Elvis poster in his right.

And thus was Reverend Robert Gray catapulted onto the national scene. Always the arbiter of right and wrong, he became an impassioned critic of American culture. Over the next few decades, as Americans embraced every perverse entertainment from Alice Cooper to *Becker* and every disquieting trend from breast implants to immodest Justice Department statuary, Gray would be there to confront the dread barbarians massing at the gate.

Indeed, he would soon become a leader in the fundamentalist movement. Until 1963, Trinity Baptist Church had been part of the Southern Baptist Convention. Gray, however, encouraged the church to break away from the convention, saying, "I could no longer endorse or approve the liberalism and modernism in the schools and encourage God's people to support it financially with tithes and offerings."

Yes, those crazy Leninist Southern Baptists and their squishy sixties moral relativism. Thank God he got out before his church became yet another Barbarellian nightmare.

A father of seven, Gray would often leave his wife at home while leading revivals across the country. Putting his faith before all else, he built Trinity into a behemoth and founded Trinity Baptist College, both of which became bellwethers in the conservative Christian movement.

For example, in a May 2006 profile on Gray, Jacksonville's *Florida Times-Union* reported on an early visit by antigay crusader Anita Bryant: "Anita Bryant brought her antigay rights campaign to Trinity Baptist in 1977. As she sat next to Gray, Bryant exhorted a group of young Sunday schoolers, many of whom looked to be 8 or 9 years old, not to mistake lust for love."

(Bryant, of course, would also become famous for such amusing bons mots as, "If gays are granted rights, next we'll have to give rights to prostitutes and to people who sleep with St. Bernards and to nail biters," and the Christastic, "We shall continue to seek help and change for homosexuals, whose sick and sad values belie the word 'gay' which they pathetically use to cover their unhappy lives.")

Still, while Gray had missed no opportunity to rebuke Satan, it turned out the two may have actually been looking for a project to do together for some time.

Fast forward to May 19, 2006. Robert Gray sits alone in a cell in Florida's Duval County Jail while being held on capital sexual battery charges. Sweet Lisa Marie, how can this be? Well, it turns out that Elvis's moral nadir—making *Clambake*—was a still a loftier attainment than Gray's own personal low point—allegedly making out with children at his Trinity Christian Academy.

As one alleged victim told Jacksonville, Florida's *First Coast News* in May of 2006, Gray allegedly became weirdly affectionate with her when she was in third grade at Trinity.

"Basically it was a make out session," recalled the then-37-year-old woman. "Sitting on his lap. Hugging. But he never put his hands where you would consider you shouldn't put your hands."

How refreshing. An old-fashioned Southern gentleman alleged pedophile.

But the accusations would get far more sordid. By July, when a former male Trinity student accused Gray of fondling him when he was 9 or 10 years old, the pastor faced several sexual battery charges.

But apparently Gray had succeeded in keeping a lid on his alleged extra-biblical activities with the help of a little spare pocket change and some well-placed threats.

One of the alleged victims recalled Gray warning, "I am like God in this church and you are just a little girl."

Another said she received a soda after she was molested, and recalled being told she was his reward.

And one said he offered her a quarter if he could kiss her using his tongue. The woman recalls thinking "this is very weird."

Yes, it was very f—ing weird. Almost too weird to be believed.

But leave it to ol' Bob to prove these kids' memories spot on. When in police custody, Gray admitted to "French kissing" several girls in his office.

Before all was said and done, at least twenty alleged victims came forward, some of whom detailed incidents far more serious than French kissing. (As of this writing, Gray is still awaiting trial on four counts of capital sexual battery.)

Now, Elvis didn't exactly have a storybook ending himself. But at worst, dying a fat dope fiend in your bathroom will get you some serious Pilates work in Purgatory. However, allegedly making out with kids is kinda off the chart—so much so that it's technically not even covered in the Bible. Although the noncanonical Gospel of Judas was rumored to have seriously frowned upon it.

And given Elvis's long ties to the town, perhaps Las Vegas should try testing out a new slogan: "What happens in Vegas . . . is not half as creepy as the alleged goings-on at Trinity Baptist Church in Jacksonville, Florida."

2.
The Fire-and-Brimstone-Spoutin', Scandal-Plagued Parson

Common Name:
Ted Haggard

Distinctive Behavior:
"Sexual immorality"; discarding street drugs

Natural Defense:
Extreme camouflage

Sometimes Confused with:
"Complete heterosexual"

It is unconscionable that the legitimate news media would report a rumor like this based on nothing but one man's accusation. Ted Haggard is a friend of mine and it appears someone is trying to damage his reputation as a way of influencing the outcome of Tuesday's election—especially the vote on Colorado's marriage-protection amendment—which Ted strongly supports.

He has shown a great deal of grace under these unfortunate circumstances, quickly turning this matter over to his church for an independent investigation. That is testament to the character I have seen him exhibit over and over again through the years.

—James Dobson, Focus on the Family

A fantasy of mine is to have an orgy with about six young college guys ranging from 18 to 22 in age.

—Ted Haggard, as recounted by Mike Jones, the male prostitute at the center of the Haggard sex scandal

As a powerful and well-respected pastor and president of the National Association of Evangelicals, Ted Haggard was for many years a key proponent of the notion that God intended one man for every woman and one woman for every man, no matter how colossal a homo you are.

In the '80s, he founded the New Life Church, which eventually grew to around 14,000 members. His large congregation and leadership of the NAE, which represented 30 million evangelicals, were big reasons why *Time* named him one of the 25 most influential evangelicals in the country.

And, naturally, Ted seemed like the ideal family man. He was married with five children and had authored several books, including *From This Day Forward: Making Your Vows Last a Lifetime, The Pursuit of the Good Life, Your Primary Purpose,* and, of course, his sole foray into children's writing, *I Love Meth and Cock.*

Yes, our story begins with Mike Jones, a gay guy just trying to get by. Young Mike could have found gainful employment at a retail store for seven bucks an hour while being forced to work weekends and holidays, or he could let other guys suck him off for a couple hundred bucks a throw. He chose the latter.

Now, you can judge all you want, but if you've ever had to fold shirts for eight hours a day at Banana Republic, you know it might be tempting to just lie back, close your eyes and count the Benjamins.

In an interview with the *Rocky Mountain News,* Jones recalled the day his life changed forever:

"*The Da Vinci Code* was out, and the History Channel was showing all these shows about it. There was one show about the Antichrist. And [Haggard] appeared as an expert. It flashed his name for a moment. I didn't catch it. But I knew right away it was him. I thought, 'Oh my God, there he is. Oh my God, that's Art.'"

Ah, the History Channel—dread nemesis to Hitler, Stalin, and gay pastors with double lives pretending to be some guy named Art.

Now, while Mike knew Art well enough, they weren't necessarily friends, per se. But they had shared things few people do. Three years before, Mike had received a call from a guy who had seen his ad on rentboy.com. Rentboy.com is a Web site where you, um, rent, uh, boys. Jones, 49, was no boy, but he was a bodybuilder and just the sort of purchase Haggard had in mind.

"He called me, saying he was visiting from Kansas City," Jones told the *Rocky Mountain News.* "We hooked up at my place. We always met at my place."

Thus began a three-year relationship, billable at $200 an hour.

Jones recalled in the *Rocky Mountain News* interview that the *Da Vinci Code* epiphany was just the beginning: "I think I was meant to know who he was because the next day I was at the gym working out about 5 A.M. Someone had put one of the TVs on Daystar, that Christian station. There he was again. I came home and went on the Internet and found out how huge he was. I thought to myself, 'Wow, this guy's big time.'"

When Jones realized what Haggard had been saying about gays and gay marriage, he began to think about exposing him. After he finally took that leap, he said, "I had to expose the hypocrisy. He is in a position of influence of millions of followers, and he's preaching against gay marriage."

Of measures that affect gays, Jones said, "Friends have suffered because of our laws. I felt obligated to get the information out about the hypocrisy of people who make these laws and those who support them.

"It may not change the way people vote, but I feel I did what I had to do. I needed to expose what was happening. You can't say one thing and do another. There are consequences to our actions."

Haggard responded to the allegations in an interview with NBC affiliate KUSA.

"I have not, I have never had a gay relationship with anybody," he said.

Of course, there was more to the story. According to Jones, Haggard apparently thought the transforming love and grace of the Lord and savior Jesus Christ might very well mix with methamphetamine like cold milk with Oreos.

At one point, Haggard asked Jones about getting meth for him. Jones explained that he didn't use the drug, but then Haggard "asked if I could hook him up I asked around and eventually gave him the name and number of someone who could supply him."

According to Jones, Haggard told him that "he loved snorting meth before [he] has sex with his wife."

Again, not something Haggard included in his book on healthy marriages.

At one point, Jones decided to start documenting his interactions with Haggard.

One saved voicemail allegedly caught Haggard apparently trying to score more drugs: "Hi Mike, this is Art. Hey, I was just calling to see if we can get any more. Either a $100 or $200 supply. And I can pick it up really anytime tomorrow, or we can wait until next week sometime. And so, I also wanted to get your address so I can send you some money for inventory. But that's obviously not working, so if you have it go ahead and get what you can. I may buzz up there. I don't know, maybe even later today, but I don't know if your schedule would allow that unless you have some in the house. So, I'll check in with you later today. Thanks, bye."

On another message, Haggard allegedly said: "Hi Mike, this is Art. Hey, I am here in Denver. Sorry that I missed you. But as I said if you want to go ahead and get the stuff then that would be great. I'll get it sometime next week or the week after or whatever. I will call you though early next week and see what is most convenient to you. Okay, thanks a lot. Bye."

The messages didn't help buttress Haggard's denials. In an interview, Haggard told KUSA, "I called him to buy some meth, but I threw it away. I bought it for myself but never used it."

Apparently, Haggard would have us believe buying crystal meth is like buying Girl Scout cookies when you're on a diet. Unfortunately, it's a little harder to give away at your weekly Oprah Book Club meeting.

Haggard would eventually confess to "sexual immorality" in a letter to his congregation, admitting, "because of pride, I began deceiving those I love the most because I didn't want to hurt or disappoint them."

Yes, it could have been pride. Or it might have been that he didn't care to tell his wife he wanted to bring home six guys from Colorado State and snort meth off their abs.

"The fact is I am guilty of sexual immorality," the letter continued. "And I take responsibility for the entire problem. I am a deceiver and a liar. There's a part of my life that is so repulsive and dark that I have been warring against it for all of my adult life."

Well, maybe it was the warring that was actually causing the trouble and not the so-called repulsive and dark stuff. Maybe if he and Jones had met when they were both in a healthier place, they might have bought a cute farmette in Vermont and raised alpacas together instead of buoying the local drug trade.

Of course, the scandal was a big blow to the evangelical movement. And coming on the heels of the Mark Foley page scandal, it no doubt further darkened the GOP's prospects in the November 2006 midterm elections.

But while Haggard had already taken a beating in the court of public opinion, the New Life Church later made its own inquiries. It uncovered a pattern of impropriety not limited to Haggard's involvement with Jones.

The Rev. Larry Stockstill summarized the findings:

"We have verified the reality of [Haggard's] struggle through numerous individuals who reported to us firsthand knowledge of everything from sordid conversation to overt suggestions to improper activities to improper relationships."

Now, what happened in the aftermath of the scandal is actually fairly instructive. Whether you regard homosexuality as a congenital trait, an acquired preference, or even a mental illness, it would be pretty silly to believe it might just evaporate overnight.

No one says, "Oh, I've loved chocolate ice cream all my life, but I went to a reeducation camp and now I hate it." Or, "Boy, I've been left-handed my whole life, but now I think lefthandedness is from the devil." Or even, "Gee, I had borderline personality disorder and generalized anxiety disorder, but I went away for two weeks and now I'm shipshape."

But for some reason, people think there's a magical, overnight cure for lack of sufficient vagina appreciation.

On February 6, 2007, the *Denver Post* reported, "The Rev. Ted Haggard emerged from three weeks of intensive counseling convinced he is 'completely heterosexual' and told an oversight board that his sexual contact with men was limited to his accuser."

Yeah. Nice. You know, it's hard to say which is more unchristian: that Haggard would betray his beliefs, his marriage, and his ministry by behaving in such a dishonest fashion to begin with, or that he apparently believes God is mentally retarded.

The paper also reported that the oversight board "strongly urged Haggard to go into secular work instead of Christian ministry if Haggard and his wife follow through on plans to earn master's degrees in psychology."

Psychology degrees? Who's writing the curriculum? Pat Robertson?

Final exam question:

How long does it take to cure homosexuality?
   a) 2 weeks
   b) 3 weeks
   c) 4 weeks
   d) Two minutes, so long as you're still allowed to have sex with 18-to-22-year-old college guys.

When asked to comment on Haggard's sudden remission, Jones said, "Well, that's the quickest therapy I've ever heard of. It's hard for me to imagine someone who is performing oral sex and saying that he is straight. That just doesn't jibe."

Yes, it's hard to believe such changes could occur in such a short time, unless they used some sort of *Clockwork Orange* technique involving pulled-back eyelids, blaring house music, and looping clips of Bruce Vilanch, Rip Taylor, and Rudy Giuliani in drag.

3. The Sunday School Spanker

Common Name:
Roger Warren Evans

Native Habitat:
Bible study class

Distinctive Behavior:
Spanking; fondling

Roger Warren Evans was a one-time prayer counselor for the Trinity Broadcasting Network and a volunteer Bible-study teacher.

For about two years in the mid-2000s, Evans taught 6-to-12-year-olds the finer points of scriptural interpretation at the Tustin, California, branch of the First Advent Christian Church.

But then he started to freelance—taking the Christian values of discipline and twisting them to his own ends.

Now, one might fairly ask what a nine-year-old Bible student could possibly do during Sunday school that would require his male teacher to take him into another room, pull down his pants, and whack his bare ass. Well, apparently, one boy would find out.

The only problem was that his teacher, Roger Evans, didn't realize that, even in the original Hebrew, the whole "spare the rod, spoil the child" bit includes nothing about giving the courtesy of a reacharound.

And so it came to pass that in March of 2006, Evans admitted to police that he had fondled the boy's genitals while spanking him, and also admitted that he had been aroused by the experience. Indeed, he was so aroused that he allegedly started inventing reasons to discipline the boy. And so the nine-year-old was treated to between 10 and 12 such sessions while attending First Advent.

While he had faced the possibility of 20 years in prison, Evans later pled guilty to lewd conduct charges and received a mere 270 days in jail and five years of probation. He is now a registered sex offender.

The rest of us are now sick to our stomachs.

4.

The Alleged May-December Unholy Trinity Croucher

Common Name:
Paul Crouch

Habitat:
Trinity Broadcasting
Network

*Also Allegedly
Frequents:*
Remote cabins with
queers (unconfirmed)

While his was almost certainly the most troubling case in the history of Trinity Broadcasting Network, Not-So-Super-Nanny Roger Warren Evans wasn't the first member of its flock to go astray.

And while James Dobson's Focus on the Family has certainly had its own problems keeping guys-gone-wild sex out of its hallowed halls, Trinity allegedly took it right to the top.

Paul Franklin Crouch is the founder and president of Trinity, which goes out to millions worldwide.

Back in the fall of 1996, when Crouch was apparently just a boy-crazy young 60-something, he allegedly had his first sexual encounter with a 30-something male employee named Enoch Lonnie Ford at a network-owned cabin near Lake Arrowhead, California.

The allegation, which Crouch has always denied, was made public when the *Los Angeles Times* reported in September 2004 that TBN had reached a $425,000 settlement six years earlier with Ford, who had threatened to sue on a claim that he'd been fired unjustly.

After that settlement was reached, Ford reportedly threatened to go public with a manuscript about the alleged affair, which his attorney had tried to exchange for $10 million.

Crouch and TBN then took legal action, obtaining a ruling that Ford could not publish without violating terms of his settlement with Trinity.

Still, questions remained. In a deposition that the *Los Angeles Times* turned up, TBN's Benny Hinn (who, keep in mind, also, according to the *London Independent,* has "preached that Adam was a superman who flew to the moon" and once said, "Sometimes I wish God would give me a Holy Ghost machine gun. I'd blow your head off!"), was quoted by a private investigator Hinn had hired as discussing "a sexual relationship that Paul Crouch had with his chauffeur," adding, "Paul's defense was that he was drunk."

Hinn denied the statements, but they were corroborated by at least one other witness.

But this isn't a group that likes to get caught with its hands in the cookie jar, much less with its hands in the pants of the guy holding the cookie jar. As histrionic defensiveness goes, Crouch could teach Bill O'Reilly a few things.

For instance, back in 1991, Crouch went after critics whom he had dismissed as "heresy hunters": "To hell with you! . . . I say get out of God's way! Quit blocking God's bridges or God's going to shoot you—if I don't!"

Heck, if it weren't for the glaring anachronism, you'd swear that was straight from the Sermon on the Mount.

5.
The Colorado Queer Chameleon

Common Name:
John Paulk

Native Habitat:
Gay bar bathrooms

Distinctive Behavior:
Fighting his own
natural urges for
Jesus

Depending on your school of thought, you may or may not believe in the malleability of sexual orientation.

But certainly, as anyone who has seen Rip Taylor knows, there are some people who are "more gay" than others. And, as with any continuum, there are distinctly different colors on this rainbow.

Well, ex-gay minister John Paulk is so far to one side of the Kinsey scale he may actually be off the visible gay spectrum—thus his insistence to his God, his ex-lesbian wife, the homosexual community, and the world at large that he is, in fact, no longer gay.

Of course, whether he's really "reformed" or has simply transcended earthly gayness to exist on some sort of celestial homosexual plane is another question entirely.

So let's take a closer look, drawing on the singular genius of Jeff Foxworthy:

- If you studied performing arts in high school and college . . . you might be a homo.

- If you had sex with men and charged them for your services . . . you might be a homo.
- If you plucked your eyebrows, put on a dress and went by the name "Candy" . . . well, you very well *might* be a homo.

And so begins the story of John Paulk, the young Ohioan who, before he found Jesus, couldn't have been any gayer if he'd been Liberace's personal bathtub attendant.

Now, it may be hard to believe, but gay John wasn't very happy with his life prior to the day he exchanged his glory holes for some glory hallelujahs. Of course, that may have less to do with living as a gay man than living as a self-destructive man-whore, but either way, the time came when he wanted to stop living life as Satan's bottom and become a red-blooded, blouse-bunny-lusting holy messenger of God.

So instead of settling down and living a normal, productive monogamous gay life, he decided to hop out of the beds of strange men into the arguably stranger bed of the ex-gay movement.

Yes, Paulk would soon find himself as chairman of and ex-gay poster child for Exodus International, the one fundamentalist religious movement that has decided not to believe in fairy tales.

Exodus International's raison d'être is to show gay men that all they really need to be happy is the love of a good ex-lesbian.

Indeed, Paulk's conversion was such a success that he and his ex-gay wife decided it was time to start bragging about it. Their story was featured on numerous national TV programs and in the pages of several widely circulated publications.

Dr. James Dobson's Focus on the Family, for which Paulk worked, also published the couple's book *Love Won Out: How God's love helped two people leave homosexuality and find each other* in which " . . . readers discover how the grace of Jesus can change any troubled heart into a new creation. The Paulks' lives are proof that no matter how far people may run from the Lord, the moment they turn around, they'll realize God's been running toward them all along."

Sadly, the Paulks would ultimately discover that it wasn't God running after them but the guy from the gay bar men's room where John had left his underwear.

On September 19, 2000, just two years after appearing on the cover of *Newsweek* with his blushing bride, John entered Mr. P's, a Washington, D.C., gay bar, while on a business trip. A patron recognized him, made some calls, and, quicker than a Paul Lynde riposte, the story was up on the Internet.

Now, the thing about reformed gay Christians is they make horrible liars. When asked why he was at a gay bar, Paulk initially claimed he had stopped in to use the bathroom.

Depending on how you look at it, he may have just been digging himself in deeper, but regardless, in the long, illustrious history of the titty bar, "I had to pee" has never really worked as an excuse for straight guys. Why would it suddenly be magic for ex-gays?

Human Rights Campaign spokesman Wayne Besen, who responded to the tip, bringing his camera in hopes of capturing a rare photo of a gay man in a gay bar, seemed a bit exasperated over the incident.

"It gets more farcical all the time," Besen said. "The Christian right has invested huge resources in promoting people like John Paulk, and now their number one spokesman, the centerpiece of their strategy, has failed. They must be asking themselves, is this a wise strategy, to pump hundreds of thousands of dollars into something that is going to end up in humiliation and embarrassment?"

Still, Focus on the Family spokeswoman Julie Niels tried to spin it as favorably as she could: "It was a significant lapse in judgment, but not a lapse in heterosexuality. We know that for sure. And one person's serious lack of judgment does not negate the fact that thousands of people have struggled out of homosexuality."

Unless Focus on the Family had equipped Paulk with a GPS monitor that flashes red in the presence of nonprocreative lust, it's hard to know how she could know anything "for sure." But as the old saying goes: You can take the boy off the farm, but he's still gonna dream about milking steers. Or something like that.

Paulk would later say, "I made a very poor decision two years ago at a low point in my life. I was having a lot of stress, and I went to an environment that used to represent something familiar and comfortable, and because of who I am, that's big news."

Um, yeah. It's big news that the one guy the Christian right holds up as an exemplar of reformed gayness finds more comfort among guys in fitted jeans and disco remixes of "It's Raining Men" than he does in the house of the Lord.

For the record, Paulk's title at FotF was Policy Analyst for Homosexuality and Gender—primarily because they couldn't agree on a font for Grand High Exalted Self-Hating Butt Pirate.

6.

The Unfocused Adulterous Trout

Common Name:
Mike Trout

Distinguishing Characteristics:
Phosphorescence
(unconfirmed)

Distinctive Behaviors:
Christian witnessing; adultery

They were dark days for Focus on the Family.

Not long after reformed gay blade John Paulk had a "lapse in judgment" and went to "use the restroom" at a Washington gay bar, the conservative Christian group faced yet another scandal.

On October 11, 2000, Mike Trout resigned as senior vice president with Focus on the Family after admitting he'd been slipping the holy spirit to someone other than his wife.

As cohost of Focus on the Family's radio show, Trout appeared to be the paragon of family values. Needless to say, his indiscretion would rock the organization.

His listeners also weighed in. One in particular said, "I'm a person who believes God really works in brokenness. Sometimes we can get too proud or think we are doing just fine. Sometimes it doesn't hurt to have a reminder we don't walk on water or glow in the dark."

Okay, the "walk on water" reference is clear, but glow in the dark? Perhaps the caller is confusing Holy Scripture with the episode where Gilligan accidentally drank the Professor's phosphorous dye.

Another caller added, "It's not like we've never heard it before. Even the best of people can have these temptations and fall into them."

Yes, we recall Focus on the Family saying the same thing about Bill Clinton.

But it was Dr. Dobson himself who provided the best punchline: "Satan has thrown just about everything in his arsenal at us in the last several weeks as you know. I am certain those who hate our cause are doing everything they can to undermine and to discredit it."

Yeah, suddenly Dana Carvey's Church Lady doesn't seem so over the top. Needless to say, convincing a former drag queen to walk into a gay bar and talking an aging radio guy into cheating on his wife hardly rank as Satan's best work. As temptations go, this is about as epic as getting Star Jones to try another piece of cheesecake.

But maybe in the end this really was all about pride. And maybe the epic pride of Dobson and his minions will finally prove their undoing. Perhaps their righteousness really is misplaced and their God will ultimately fail to protect them from Satan's wiles.

And maybe, when all is said and done, they will be turned away from the kingdom of God, where the virtuous walk on water and righteous men glow in the dark.

7.

The Antiporn Pastoral Pair

Common Name:
Bradley Hoefs/
Michael Hintz

Distinctive Call:
Porn is bad

Distinctive Behavior:
Preaching,
practicing,
perving out

When the conservative Christian group Omaha for Decency ran a full-page ad in the July 9, 2000, edition of the *Omaha World-Herald,* the message was clear: ixnay on the ornpay.

The "Open Letter of Concern Regarding Obscenity in Our Community" was signed by area pastors convinced that the legal sale of adult pornography was harming the residents of Omaha.

As proof, they cited some of the very latest research, including a 23-year-old *Psychology Today* article titled "Sexual Murderers."

Sure, just a few years before the article ran, the American Psychiatric Association still listed homosexuality as a mental disorder, but these upstanding men and women would not be deterred. They answered God's call to stanch the flow of totally awesome adult entertainment.

Sadly, in about six years moderately intelligent nine-year-olds would be able to download Larry Flynt's life's work in the time it took their mothers to walk out to the mailbox with their monthly Focus on the Family checks, but in the summer of 2000 it still looked like the tide might turn if only www.brazilianshemales.com could be banished from public library computers in portions of Nebraska.

One of the pastors who signed the Omaha for Decency ad was Bradley Hoefs. Ironically, just five years earlier, Hoefs was charged with exposing himself to an undercover police officer. Now, in case you think he might have been just some random horny guy who was spotted by an overzealous cop slapping the ham to a grainy Jenna Jameson pic in private, the *World-Herald* reported that, according to the police report, Hoefs "masturbated while exposing himself to the officer." He was ultimately convicted of indecent exposure. This hardly seems like the kind of guy who should be criticizing other men for renting *Bikini Carwash Company 2*.

Of course, Hoefs denied the charges, but he did resign his post at King of Kings Lutheran Church. Always one to land on his feet, he soon thereafter became pastor of Community of Grace Church.

But Omaha for Decency's troubles were just beginning.

Enter Michael Hintz.

Hintz was a pastor at Trinity Church Interdenominational when he signed the antiporn advert. He eventually moved to Des Moines, Iowa, where he became a youth pastor for the First Assembly of God Church. But he couldn't escape the curse that followed him from Omaha.

On October 4, 2004, President Bush spoke at the South Suburban YMCA in Des Moines to promote his tax-cut plan. The speech was a carefully designed piece of political stagecraft, with a bit of bad—as in really, really, *really* bad—casting. (Imagine Meryl Streep's role in *Sophie's Choice* going to, say, Jim Nabors.)

"The money they keep will make it easier to save for their retirement, or their children's education, invest in a home or a small business, or pay off credit card debts," said Bush. "One of those families is the Hintz family, from Clive, Iowa."

Indeed, the Hintzes were the idyllic family in Bush's America:

a middle-class youth pastor, his wife, and four children, all of whom love Jesus, their country, and supply-side tax cuts.

"It's a special day for Mike and Sharla, not because they're with the president . . . but because it's their thirteenth wedding anniversary. Theirs is a typical story. See, last year they received a child tax credit check for $1,600 for their four children. And under all the tax relief we've passed they saved about $2,800 last year. With this extra money they bought a wood-burning stove to reduce their home heating costs. They made a decision for their family.

"They also made home repairs and improvements. They took the family on a vacation to Minnesota. Next year when you get your check, you may want to come to Texas. Without the tax bill I'm signing today, the Hintzes would have paid $1,200 more in federal taxes next year. Think about that. Here's a family of four, working hard to raise their kids, the money would have been going out of their pocket. I believe they can spend that $1,200 better than the federal government can."

Yeah, George was wrong on that one.

Less than a month after Bush's speech, Hintz was fired from the First Assembly of God after being accused of having a sexual relationship with a teenager.

He was arrested in December and charged with sexual exploitation by a counselor, and in March 2005 pleaded guilty to the charges.

8.
The Canadian Migrating Jesus Screamer

Common Name:
Jonathan Bell

Distinctive Calls:
High-pitched
shriek; self-effacing
wail

Natural Habitats:
Texas; Canada;
cable TV

Natural Enemies:
Demons

In the vast pantheon of televangelists you'll find some true freaks, but none quite as riveting as Jonathan Bell.

If you ever watched *The Daily Show* in the days before Jon Stewart, when Craig Kilborn was host and John Bloom's "God Stuff" segment was all the rage, then you probably remember Bell.

After the show played several clips of Bell ranting at the top of his lungs, he became something of a cult figure.

Now, it's not like Bell would occasionally scream out a word or phrase for emphasis. Oh, no. That's commonplace among evangelical preachers, and more or less to be expected.

No, the best way to describe him is that if Pat Robertson and Sam Kinison had a love child, it would be Jonathan Bell.

This was a man who expressed his deepest, most heartfelt religious convictions with a mixture of taunting, self-loathing, and shrieking, crimson-faced hate.

Now, while most book publishers would normally not sanction such a liberal helping of uppercase letters, there's really no other way to convey the man's tone. So please bear with us.

Here's Bell:

"I MEAN I GAVE UP MY BUSINESS IN CANADA TWO YEARS AGO! A HUNDRED THOUSAND DOLLARS A YEAR SALARY TO COME IN TO THE MINISTRY WHERE I'M NOT EVEN MAKING FIFTEEN GRAND A YEAR!"

Of course, at other times the public was treated to a more subdued Bell, telling us more details than we could reasonably be expected to process about his depressing life:

"Do you know when I came into this ministry two and a half years ago, my whole family disowned me? My girlfriend left me. My friends left me. My whole staff of my business quit on me overnight and my phone stopped ringing. And I had demons visiting me daily for two weeks."

Yeah, no one else knows what he's talking about, either, but that's hardly the point. The fact is this man left his comfortable life in Canada to come to Dallas, Texas, where he hoped to find a seller's market for screeching biblical scholarship. And make no mistake about it, Bell's message was a fundamentalist conservative one:

"HOMOSEXUALS AREN'T HAPPY TODAY! THEY GO TO BARS, THEY'RE LOOKING FOR LOVE! THERE'S NO LOVE IN A GAY BAR! NO LOVE!!! AND YOU KNOW IT!!!!!"

"GOD WANTS YOU TO COME INTO ONENESS WITH HIM! YOUR BODY IS NOT MEANT TO BE WITH ANOTHER MAN! And I'm a prime example of that."

Well, it turned out that Bell was right when he said he was struggling with demons. A December 1998 article in the *Ottawa Sun* detailed some of his more troubling run-ins with Satan:

"A man convicted of sex crimes against children who runs a hairdressing salon in Rockland denies he disobeyed a court order by advertising makeovers for kids.

"Jonathan Bell, 39, was convicted of three counts of sexual interference in December 1995 against two 12-year-old boys he met while working at a Kingston salon.

"After serving 14 months in a Kingston jail he was released and placed on two years probation and order[ed] to receive treatment at the Royal Ottawa Hospital.

"But Bell maintains he didn't breach a separate court order stipulating no contact with children under the age of 14 until the year 2001. The order, he said, allows him to be around children if supervised by another adult.

"'You can't throw me into the same basket [as convicted pedophiles],' Bell told the *Sun* yesterday. 'I don't prey on children. I understand what I did was wrong, but it will never happen again. That is part of my past.'"

Perhaps amid all his wild rantings, Jonathan Bell said it best:

"You know, it's very easy to preach the word on Sunday and live like the devil through the week."
    Indeed.

9.

The Great Sobbing Swaggart

Common Name:
Jimmy Swaggart

Native Habitats:
Christian television
and radio

Distinctive Call:
"I'm gonna kill him
and tell God he
died"

Mating Habits:
Ministering
to prostitutes

It's one thing when a high-profile public figure gets caught in a compromising situation after decades spent preaching furiously against adultery, homosexuality, and perversion.

That's what's referred to in Republican PR circles as "the #5."

But it takes a pair of real Christ-like cajones to get caught with a hooker and then, just a few short years later, start talking endless shit about *other* people's relationships.

On September 12, 2004, televangelist Jimmy Swaggart was ranting away on Canadian television when he said this: "I get amazed at these politicians dancing around this. I'm trying to find the correct name for it . . . this utter absolute, asinine, idiotic stupidity of men marrying men."

He added, "I've never seen a man in my life I wanted to marry."

Yeah, and most of us have never seen a street hooker we'd like to take back to a motel room that couldn't pass a black light inspection if Forest Service firefighters hosed it down with Clorox and hydrogen peroxide, but that's maybe beside the point.

Indeed, Jimmy Swaggart, the man best known for his face-melting apology after being outed in a prostitution scandal back in the late '80s, apparently thought, a mere decade and a half later, that he finally had the whole sexual ethics thing down pat—and, significantly, it included neither Adam nor Steve.

Now, that Jimmy Swaggart has never met a man he wanted to marry (though it's curious that the comment sort of implies that it could conceivably happen someday) really doesn't prove anything. It's fairly rare that someone would be walking down the street, minding his or her business, see someone of the same sex and suddenly think, "Wow, I want to marry *that*."

But that's apparently the world Christian conservatives live in—a primordial hormone soup where sexuality is so mutable we need to put gay-sex shock collars on the populace to prevent people from straying from the hetero yard.

But Swaggart was just getting warmed up. It wasn't enough that their lifestyle had doomed them to perdition, homosexuals also had a self-deputized sex sheriff to worry about:

"And I'm gonna be blunt and plain; if one ever looks at me like that, I'm gonna kill him and tell God he died."

Say, is that the Contemporary English or King James version?

Now, it's really quite amusing that crazy, frothing homophobes who look like Jimmy Swaggart always seem to think that gay men are trying desperately to get in their pants. To think that every gay man is attracted to every other man is a little like assuming straight men fantasize in equal numbers about Angelina Jolie and Ruth Buzzi. While a young man who's confused about his sexuality might find himself thinking about Ricky Martin, he most likely won't imagine heavy petting with Colonel Sanders or Hugh Downs.

But even funnier is that Swaggart apparently thinks he can play three-card monte with the omniscient creator of the universe—killing queers and driving through seedy areas of town looking for whores right under the Almighty's nose.

But while Swaggart appeared to be saying "hate the sin, kill the sinner," he was not completely hard-hearted. In a moment of empathy, he also said, "I'm not knocking the poor homosexuals."

Well, that's a relief. Imagine if he *were* knocking homosexuals. He might even start talking about killing them.

Strangely, though, when it came to his own sin, he was a lot quicker to forgive.

Back in '88, after his highly publicized scandal had basically turned him into the Pets.com of the moral authority biz, he stood chastened before his flock and kinda sorta apologized.

"I do not plan in any way to whitewash my sin," said Swaggart.

He added, "No one is to blame but Jimmy Swaggart."

Yes, you can always tell when someone truly owns their actions—they start speaking in the third person.

"I take the responsibility. I take the blame. I take the fall."

Interesting choice of words. It was almost like he was starting to move, by degrees, further and further away from responsibility.

Rarely does someone say they are taking the fall for something they're 100 percent responsible for. (Remember Jeffrey Dahmer "taking the fall" for those murders?) No, usually you "take the fall" when there's plenty of blame to go around, but it's easier to scapegoat one individual.

Of course, a source who talked to a Jimmy Swaggart World Ministries board member also pointed out that Swaggart didn't quite get past third base with his prostitute, saying he only paid her to perform pornographic acts.

Okay, that's actually fifty times creepier than just banging a hooker. Why is it that whenever a conservative preacher decides to finally release his id, it's always got to involve an eggplant and a Portuguese horse tranquilizer or something? For God's sake, just have a friggin' affair.

"I have asked myself 10,000 times through 10,000 tears. Maybe Jimmy Swaggart has tried to live his entire life as though he was not human . . ."

Again with the third person. You know, Jimmy, that was actually you with that hooker. But if you really want to think of yourself as a pathetic supporting character in a dark tragicomedy, go ahead. You certainly won't be alone.

10.
The Philandering Lord-Praising Bakker

Common Name:
Jim Bakker

Distinctive Behaviors:
Hoarding; adultery

Distinctive Call:
"Praise the Lord!"

Status:
Roaming free
in Missouri

The Jim Bakker PTL scandal is rightly regarded as the *Godfather* of Christian conservative sex scandals. It broke new ground, created tremendous buzz, and was widely imitated.

Indeed, it's easy to imagine Ted Haggard, tears in his eyes, giving a heartfelt tribute to a doddering, silver-haired Bakker at a Kennedy Center Honors ceremony for lifetime achievement twenty or so years from now: "You made it possible for all of us, man. I love ya. Jesus loves ya. We can't thank you enough. All of us. If I weren't completely heterosexual, I'd give you a big, wet kiss. And maybe a happy ending. Who knows? That was weird. I know. Sorry. God bless."

Jim and Tammy Faye Bakker started broadcasting from an old furniture store back in 1974, but by the '80s the ministry had grown into a multimillion-dollar enterprise. The money flowed liberally, and the Bakkers became notorious for their cupidity.

Now, greed and lust are two things that don't go over real well with ol' J.C., but the

Bakkers, like many birds of a feather in their flock, tended to forget that from time to time.

The Jim Bakker scandal was, of course, two-pronged. The more serious and less interesting part involved fraud and a prison term related to his ministry.

But it was his famous encounter with church secretary Jessica Hahn that really brought the walls of Jericho a-tumblin' down.

It snowballed from there and eventually the whole thing got weirder than the late Tammy Faye's short-lived mid-'90s talk show with Jim J. Bullock.

Oh, but this is America, where Christian forgiveness and prurient curiosity conspire to give new life to practically anyone with a story to sell.

In July of 2006, the *Kansas City Star* caught up with Bakker and reported that he had purchased a plot in that quintessentially American graveyard of talent, fame, and human dignity, Branson, Missouri:

"Bakker, who settled in Branson three years ago, has quietly rebuilt a following and his life.

"He and his second wife, Lori Graham Bakker, are hosts of the hourlong *Jim Bakker Show* on about 50 stations nationwide. It recently started showing on DirecTV. The show will move to a larger location south of Branson in about six months.

"'It's a miracle what's happened here, it's an absolute miracle,' Bakker told his audience."

Miracle?

Yeah, somehow it's hard to believe God woke up one morning in 2003, beheld his creation and said, "Well, it's 9 A.M. I've got time to either cure a couple million Third World kids of deadly dysentery and malaria, or I can get Bakker that gig in Branson. Hmmm, let's go with Bakker. The kid's paid his dues."

11.
The White-Collared, Boy-Diddling Clerics

Common Name:
Catholic Clergy

Distinctive Behaviors:
Touchy feely . . .
and not in the
emotional way

Native Habitat:
In grand houses
of worship

*Distinguishing Char-
acteristics:*
Long white dress
with a smokin'
hand bag

The roots of Christian attitudes toward sex go back hundreds of years, stretching from St. Paul's apparent discomfort with sexuality to the priestly celibacy requirement to the modern Catholic proscriptions on birth control.

Author Charles Freeman gives a snapshot of that history in his book *The Closing of the Western Mind:* "One of the results of the elevation of virginity was to transform women who did not espouse it into temptresses, the 'dancing girls' of Jerome's vision. While Mary was contrasted with Eve, women as a whole were equated with Eve, perpetuating her guilt through the temptation they offer to men. 'Do you not realize that Eve is you?' inveighed the tempestuous Tertullian. 'The curse God pronounced on your sex weighs still on the world. . . . You are the devil's gateway, you desecrated the fatal tree, you first betrayed the law of God, you who softened up with your cajoling words the man against whom the devil could not prevail by force. . . .'"

Now, while the Holy See is the rightful purveyor and protector of Church doctrine and history—and thus it might seem presumptuous for mere scribblers to weigh in on such matters—it would be safe to say that Tertullian desperately needed to get his piston lubed.

But if the Church's history of sexual repression had simply led to a bitter nun here or there, it might have been of little note. But many would argue that it's ultimately helped create the biggest scandal in our entire countdown.

Now, trying to write a comprehensive profile on the Catholic Church priest pedophilia scandal would be beyond Herculean.

Indeed, it would be a little like trying to count the grains of sand in the desert—if dozens of bishops were constantly scooping the sand up and placing it in administrative jobs where it would no longer be in contact with children.

Of course, some church apologists have tried to dismiss reports of priestly sexual abuse as merely anecdotal—the result of over-zealous media. They will argue that sexual abuse is a problem endemic to society as a whole, and is not unique to the church.

That's no doubt true. For instance, only 50 percent of the authors of this book went to a school whose priest was later forced to resign for an incident of sexual abuse that had occurred before he was assigned to the parish. (The other 50 percent went to public school.)

But what of the much-cited June 2002 story in the *Dallas Morning News* that reported that two-thirds of American bishops had allowed priests accused of sexual abuse to stay in their ministries? Rome's official response is instructive and lends much-needed perspective to the . . . wait, *two-thirds? Two fucking thirds? Jesus Foxtrottin' Christ on a Motor Scooter, are you fucking kidding with this?* Costco sporting goods managers have more goddamn sense.

Anyway, instead of trying to track down all the priests and bishops who have been tainted by scandal—which would be prohibitively labor-intensive and would only serve to further trauma-tize former victims, who may as a result find themselves caught up in embarrassing impromptu games of Six Degrees of Bishop Weakland—the authors prefer to take the enormity of the crisis as read.

As for the seemingly systemic nature of the problem, the following excerpt from Thomas P. Doyle, A.W. Richard Sipe, and Patrick Wall's *Sex, Priests, and Secret Codes: The Catholic Church's 2,000-Year Paper Trail of Sexual Abuse* is instructive.

In a section called "Cult of Systemic Secrecy," the authors write:

"This aura of secrecy is nurtured by the church. The oath that cardinals take, for instance, never to divulge anything confided to them that 'might bring harm or dishonor to Holy Church' creates a template for everybody else to keep scandals under wraps. The oath reads: 'I [name] cardinal of the Holy Roman Church, promise and swear to remain, from this moment and for as long as I live, faithful to Christ and his gospel, constantly obedient to the Holy Apostolic Roman Church, to the Blessed Peter in the person of the Supreme Pontiff [name] and of his successors canonically elected; to preserve always in word and deed communion with the Catholic Church; never to reveal to anyone whatsoever has been confided to me to keep secret and the revelation of which could cause damage or dishonor to the Holy Church; to carry out with great diligence and fidelity the tasks to which I am called in my service to the Church, according to the norms of law. So help me Almighty God.'

"When one bishop was chided by a priest for denying the existence of sexual abuse when he did, in fact, know about it, he replied: 'I only lie when I have to.' And as recently as May 2002, a judge of the Holy Roman Rota, the highest court in the church, wrote in a Vatican-approved article that bishops should not report sexual violations of priests to civil authorities. The reasoning: lest the image and authority of the church be compromised and victims harmed instead of protected."

Beautiful.

Somewhere, St. Peter and George Orwell just high-fived each other.

DIDJAKNOW?

Long rumored to be gay, and portrayed as such in Tony Kushner's Pulitzer Prize–winning play *Angels in America,* Roy Cohn died in August 1986 of AIDS. The chief aide to Republican Senator Joseph McCarthy during his infamous pursuit of alleged communists, Cohn had consistently claimed to be suffering from liver cancer.

The Kid in Your Closet:
Gay Children of Prominent Conservatives

If some conservatives are to be believed, there's no greater threat to our republic or the vitality of Western civilization itself than boys who wanna kiss other boys.

It's the plank in their platform that, ironically, appears to have the most wood.

So there's nothing that sends a Republican pol into screaming-queen mode quite like a queer son or daughter—unless it's a frozen embryo living in an impeccably furnished cryonic chamber with an antique Queen Anne tea service and a complete collection of Pet Shop Boys albums.

You almost feel sorry for these people. They spend the bulk of their careers droning on and on about the deviance of homosexuality—how it's an illegitimate choice, not a biologi-cally determined orientation—and then, lo and behold, God blesses them with a big gay bundle of joy. They're either forced to concede that they've utterly failed to instill a moral sense in their children or that their exclusive country-club gene pool is actually a rank cesspool of immorality.

Most of the time, their public reactions range from inadequate to downright shameful. Some try to support their kids privately but continue to pander to their religious conservative base by signing onto public policy that denies them basic rights.

Following are a few of the more notable Republican homo-spawners who have tried to walk that vanishingly thin tightrope between their love of family and their love of the gay-bashing vote.

MARY, THE AMAZING SECRET CORPORATE GAY LIAISON

One of the odder moments in the 2004 presidential campaign was Lynne Cheney's reaction to John Kerry's "outing" of Mary Cheney, the openly gay daughter of Vice President Dick Cheney.

During an October 2004 debate with George W. Bush, Kerry responded to a question on whether homosexuality is a choice with the answer that dare not speak its name: "We're all God's children. . . . And I think if you were to talk to Dick Cheney's daughter, who is a lesbian, she would tell you that she's being who she was, she's being who she was born as. I think if you talk to anybody, it's not a choice."

The Cheneys were indignant. How dare Kerry mention that their daughter Mary, who once worked as the gay/lesbian corporate relations manager for Coors and who once, as part of her duties, toured the country with the winner of the International Mr. Leather 1999 competition, was gay?

Said Dick's wife, Lynne: "This is not a good man. And of course, I am speaking as a mom and a pretty indignant mom. This is not a good man. What a cheap and tawdry political trick."

For his part, Dick said that Kerry "will say and do anything in order to get elected. . . . And I am not speaking just as a father here, though I am a pretty angry father, but as a citizen."

Now, it would be naive to claim that Kerry *wasn't* trying to paint the Bush administration into a corner by pointing out their abundant hypocrisy over gay rights.

After all, the administration had, earlier that year, declared its support for a constitutional amendment that would ban gay marriage. A *New York Times* story on Bush's announcement reported, "Republicans said Mr. Bush was also seeking to draw a sharp distinction between himself and the Democratic front-runner in the primaries, Senator John Kerry of Massachusetts."

Cheney did break from the administration philosophically—saying he believed gay marriage should be a state issue—but in the end he deferred to his president:

"At this point, my own preference is as I've stated," Cheney said. "But the president makes basic policy for this administration, and he's made it clear that he does in fact support a constitutional amendment on this issue."

So if anything, the Cheneys should have been applauding Kerry, who actually embraced Mary Cheney's sexuality, instead of hoping to conceal their daughter's orientation from their antigay conservative base. Indeed, the way they talked about Mary, you'd think she was a vacuous Texas party girl or a strung-out silver-spoon drug addict who'd been charged with prescription fraud.

For instance, in 2000, Lynne Cheney went so far as to deny that Mary had declared herself a lesbian, even though she had been the go-to gay at Coors, and had worked to persuade gay rights leaders to end their support for a boycott of the company.

"Mary has never declared such a thing," said Lynne in an interview with ABC's Cokie Roberts. "I would like to say that I'm appalled at the media interest in one of my daughters."

In 2007, in an interview with CNN's Wolf Blitzer, Dick Cheney, who contributed chromosomes 24 through 46 to the Cheney family gayborg, took exception when the topic of his inconveniently gay daughter reared its head.

(Note: The following transcript doesn't do the interview justice. You really need a visual. Probably the best way to describe it is that Cheney came about as close as a man can to devouring the head of another human being without actually following through.)

> *Blitzer:* We're out of time, but a couple of issues I want to raise with you. Your daughter Mary, she's pregnant. All of us are happy. She's going to have a baby. You're going to have another grandchild. Some of the—some critics, though, are suggesting, for example, a statement from someone representing Focus on the Family: "Mary Cheney's pregnancy raises the question of what's best for children. Just because it's possible to conceive a child outside of the relationship of a married mother and father, doesn't mean it's best for the child." Do you want to respond to that?

Cheney: No, I don't.

Blitzer: She's obviously a good daughter . . .

Cheney: I'm delighted—I'm delighted I'm about to have a sixth grandchild, Wolf, and obviously think the world of both of my daughters and all of my grandchildren. And I think, frankly, you're out of line with that question.

Blitzer: I think all of us appreciate . . .

Cheney: I think you're out of—I think you're out of line with that question.

Blitzer: . . . your daughter. We like your daughters. Believe me, I'm very, very sympathetic to Liz and to Mary. I like them both. That was just a question that's come up and it's a responsible, fair question.

Cheney: I just fundamentally disagree with your perspective.

Translation: If you're boarding an airliner anytime in the next year or so and you see Wolf Blitzer in line with you, you might want to look into booking a later flight.

Of course, one wonders how Dick and Lynne Cheney might have reacted if one of their daughters had openly declared a fondness for mountain climbing, or Dippin' Dots Ice Cream, or even Celine Dion. There are really only two possible responses: It's a shameful thing that has to be talked about in shameful whispers, or it's an ordinary, acceptable preference that can be openly discussed.

But the Cheneys prefer to walk an uncomfortable middle ground where, when asked, they profess to love with all their hearts their degenerate little sin blossom.

While Mary herself seemed to agree that Kerry was out of line in mentioning her glaringly obvious homosexuality to, well, people, most gays seemed to line up behind Kerry who, after all, wasn't treating their orientation like an X-Men mutation.

"What's tawdry, and what they should be angry about, is the Republican Party's overt and ugly smears of all gay people including, therefore, [their own] daughter," said Matt Foreman, executive director of the National Gay and Lesbian Task Force. "They ought to call off their buddies on the radical right who cannot talk about gay people without also talking about pedophilia, bestiality, and molestation [instead of choosing] the party and this partisan game-playing over their own child."

Well, jeez, when you put it that way . . .

SONNY AND QUEER

Sometime between using his young daughter as a stage prop in his wildly popular '70s variety show and crashing his head into a tree, entertainer-turned-congressman Sonny Bono cosponsored the Defense of Marriage Act, a notorious antigay bill signed into law by Bill Clinton in 1996.

Turns out cute little Chastity, the daughter in question, was a lesbo-in-waiting.

Even though Chastity Bono claimed it was Sonny who was more supportive when she came out than was her mother, Cher, Bono's antigay politics did create a rift between father and daughter.

"He was a Republican politician in the 104th Congress, which had a very conservative freshman class, and I think he did what he thought he had to do to stay in office," Chastity told reporter Nancy Murrell in an interview conducted months after her father's death.

Nevertheless, Bono's wish to maintain a good relationship with his constituents inevitably soured his relationship with his daughter.

"I took it very personally," Chastity told the gay periodical *The Advocate*. "It put a tremendous amount of distance between us, and then he died before we were able to resolve it."

Indeed, the distance between the two forced Chastity to do a

Deuteronomy double-dip, leading her already abomination-sullied soul to seek answers in the occult.

Though Chastity's half-sister, Christy, had tried to bring Sonny and Chastity together to resolve the issue of her getting her lesbianism on his politics and him getting his politics on her lesbianism, the summit never happened.

"Medium James Van Praagh did a reading with my mother recently and one of the things he said to her was that my dad said, 'I wish I listened to Christy. I should have called Chas,'" said Chastity.

While trusting the word of a psychic might not be the best way to go, it's nice that Van Praagh could bring some peace to Sonny Bono's innocent young daughter. Unfortunately, it's no substitute for your father not being a prick when he's alive.

KEYES TO LESBIAN HEAVEN

Alan Keyes is a far-right Republican and moral crusader best known for a couple of anemic presidential primary runs and a 2004 Illinois Senate race through which he achieved a measure of public approval normally reserved for food-borne pathogens.

In August of 2004, he became notorious in LGBT circles for referring to Mary Cheney as a "selfish hedonist."

Alas, it was the fatherly equivalent of the baseball fan who loudly proclaims that his favorite team's pitcher is working on a no-hitter.

Less than six months later, Keyes' own daughter Maya was telling anyone who would listen (which, apparently, included her father) that she herself was gay.

It posed as stark a choice between familial love and rock-ribbed ideology as any human being would ever likely face.

Guess which choice Alan Keyes made.

Sadly, you'd be right.

The Washington Post reported that Maya's parents had thrown her out of the house, stopped speaking to her, and refused to pay for her college education because of her sexual orientation.

The Gay That Won't Go Away

In a December 2003 column posted on the Web site of the Eagle Forum, a conservative "pro-family" organization she founded in 1972, renowned antifeminist and right-wing activist Phyllis Schlafly wrote the following in defense of traditional marriage:

"Since the Massachusetts Supreme Court ruled in favor of same-sex marriages in *Goodridge v. Dept. of Public Health,* reporters have been asking presidential candidates for their comment. Their unresponsive answers reveal their hope that the issue will recede before the 2004 elections.

"But the issue won't go away, and every candidate might as well get prepared with a coherent answer. The gay rights lobby smells political victory, and the majority of Americans are digging in to protect a fundamental prop of civilization.

"Whining about discrimination, the gay lobby is trying to position the Massachusetts ruling as a logical expansion of the civil rights movement. It isn't.

"No one has the right to marry whomever he wants. Gays can already get marriage licenses on exactly the same terms as anyone else.

"Everyone is equally barred from marrying another person who is under a certain age, or too closely related, or of the same gender, or already married to another. Sound reasons underlie all these requirements, which apply equally to everyone, male and female."

Phyllis Schlafly is, of course, the proud owner of a gay son.

Pete Knight, the Homo Slayer

If there's a gold-medal winner in the Republican gay-kid Olympiad, it's state Senator William "Pete" Knight of California.

Senator Knight was the author of California's Proposition 22, which banned gay marriage in the state after passing with more than 60 percent of the vote in 2000.

In March of 2004, his son, David Knight, wed his partner, Joe Lazzaro, in a San Francisco ceremony just a month after Senator Knight called the city's same-sex marriages "nothing more than a sideshow."

But this was no mere case of mistaken identity. The elder Knight had known for years of his son's sexual orientation before crafting his antigay marriage referendum.

As one might expect, the younger Knight would become something of a gay hero.

According to a story in the *San Francisco Chronicle:* "Knight's stand against his father in 2000 is well known within the gay community. When [deputy marriage commissioner Donald] Bird, the volunteer who performed Tuesday's ceremony, learned afterward who he had just wed, he gasped.

"'You are giving me goosebumps,' he said. 'I just married Pete Knight's son.'"

Section III
Conservativicus Debaucheria

You don't have to be elected to public office or work behind a pulpit to be involved in a sex scandal anymore. Really, it's true. Now all social conservatives are more than welcome to the party. Whether you're an antigay spokesman or an abortion-clinic protestor, there's plenty of room for you in the big comfy bed of right-wing debauchery. Just leave your moral compass and your pants at the door.

This final section looks at the sideline lurkers in the conservative movement—those who aren't necessarily first-stringers in the political game, but who love looking up the skirts of cheerleaders nonetheless.

1.

The Fetus-Protectin' Clumsy Molester

Common Name:
John Allen Burt

Native Habitat:
Protesting outside
abortion clinics

Mating Habits:
Accidentally falling
on young girls

Those who would presume to act as the arbiters of morality walk a dangerous path indeed.

After all, most of us who have lived in the real world and faced its myriad challenges know that there are relatively few moral absolutes.

Oh, but here's one: If you ever decide to dedicate your life to stopping teenage girls from having abortions and then later start a home to help unwed mothers transition into motherhood, you should not, under any circumstances, attempt to have sex with them.

Case in point: John Allen Burt.

Johnny B. loved fetuses. He loved them so much, in fact, that he went to extremes to protect them. Back in 1991, John bought land adjacent to a health clinic in Pensacola, Florida, that performed abortions. He then used that land to launch protests. He also disseminated information about abortion doctors.

After one of Burt's associates, Michael Griffin, shot a doctor, David Gunn, at a demonstration, the Gunn family sued him.

Later, in 1994, Paul Hill, another associate of Burt's, killed Dr. John Britton and a clinic escort in Pensacola.

It soon became apparent that the body count was escalating a little too quickly for even a fringe pro-life faction, and, after giving up his protesting turf in a settlement with the Gunn family, Burt told the *Pensacola News-Journal* that he would be turning his focus to his home for 12-to-17-year-old girls.

Now that sounded like a better use of everyone's time.

Unfortunately, it would soon be made clear that John Allen Burt had about as much business being head of a home for girls as Janice Dickinson had being chief of neurosurgery at Johns Hopkins.

It turns out that disturbingly zealous abortion protests were not the chick magnet he thought they'd be, and he apparently reasoned that taking advantage of hopeless teen girls going through traumatic pregnancies would be an easier way to score.

And so it was that, by early June 2003, Burt found himself on the run from his home for unwed girls, the creepily named Our Father's House.

Karen Krzan, Burt's daughter, said her father went missing in the early evening of June 5, when, wrote the *St. Petersburg Times,* "he fell on the 15-year-old girl near the kitchen in his home, got up, walked out and drove off." The paper also wrote that Krzan claimed the allegations stemmed "from Burt's fall on the girl and nothing else."

Now, the "I just fell on top of her by accident" defense would be tough for any lawyer to pull off. *Maybe* Denny Crane could do it, but he'd need a sympathetic jury made up of at least seven other fringe pro-life activists who had been accused of assault after accidentally falling on teen girls.

But despite his daughter's daffy theory, it turned out that John Burt had been investigated before on similar charges, though police never had enough evidence to issue an arrest warrant. This time the investigation yielded four charges: one count of lewd and lascivious conduct and three counts of lewd and lascivious molestation. (To this day, the charge of accidentally falling on someone has yet to be filed by the DA's office.)

And Burt, like all innocent people who accidentally bump into other people, fled the scene and was apprehended a few days later in his dark green Chevy van.

Burt would ultimately get 18 years in prison for his work with unwed teen mothers. He would also later lose an appeal.

So here's another moral absolute: If you're a conservative guy and you ever find yourself accidentally falling on a teenage girl you're trying to help, you should probably try to avoid groping her before you get up off the floor. It's just better for everyone that way.

2.

The Bush-Dwellin', Butt-Lovin' Hager

Common Name:
David Hager

Distinctive Behaviors:
Opposing birth-control; developing own unique birth-control methods

Distinctive Call:
"God has used me to stand in the breach"

Status:
Extremely divorced

In the long history of human civilization, from the first nascent agrarian settlements in the Fertile Crescent to the release of the film *Chasing Liberty* and beyond, it's safe to assume that very few men have anally penetrated their wives in their sleep.

No matter what Hobbesian brutalities the coarser sex has visited upon women over the years—and there have been many—those who have anally penetrated their wives in their sleep almost certainly comprise a vanishingly small fraternity. A good guess is that they're no more than .002 percent of the population. There's no Zogby polling data to confirm this, but let's just take it as a commonsense ballpark figure.

So when one does stumble across a bona fide case of a man anally penetrating his wife in her sleep, there would ordinarily be no reason to think, "No, no, not strange enough. We gotta make that story punchier."

Oh, but this is a nonfiction book. And you know what they say about nonfiction.

Dr. David Hager was a respected OB/GYN,

a member of Focus on the Family's Physician Resource Council, and a member of the FDA's Advisory Committee for Reproductive Health Drugs.

As a member of the committee (and a Bush appointee), he became a strong advocate against the morning-after pill.

Of course, his stances on this and other issues brought criticism from liberals and reproductive rights advocates, and as a result he felt aggrieved.

In October 2004, in a sermon at Asbury College, a nondenominational Christian school in Kentucky, he spoke of the persecution he and other Christians had endured.

"You see . . . there is a war going on in this country," he said. "And I'm not speaking about the war in Iraq. It's a war being waged against Christians, particularly evangelical Christians. It wasn't my scientific record that came under scrutiny (at the FDA). It was my faith. . . . By making myself available, God has used me to stand in the breach."

Unfortunately, it wasn't just the breach he wanted to stand in.

You see, his objection to the morning-after pill actually made lots of sense. It was a drug he saw little need for, as he had allegedly been anally sodomizing his narcoleptic wife for years.

In a May 2005 interview with *The Nation,* Hager's ex-wife, Linda, shed new light on the couple's 32-year marriage. The bad news was he had anally sodomized his narcoleptic wife as she slept; the good news was he only did it for seven years, or a little more than 20 percent of their time together.

Not surprisingly, David and Linda had widely different takes on their relationship.

"In early 2002," said Hager in his Asbury sermon, "my world fell apart. . . . After thirty-two years of marriage, I was suddenly alone in a new home that we had built as our dream home. Time spent 'doing God's will' had kept me from spending the time I needed to nourish my marriage."

Apparently, that speech was too much for Linda to handle, and she blew the lid off his unusual habits.

"I probably wouldn't have objected so much, or felt it was so abusive if he had just wanted normal sex all the time," she told *The Nation*. "But it was the painful, invasive, totally nonconsensual nature of the sex that was so horrible."

"My sense is that he saw [my narcolepsy] as an opportunity," she added.

Oh, but if only the ironies had ended there. In his book *As Jesus Cared for Women*, Hager wrote, "Even though I was trained as a medical specialist, it wasn't until I began to see how Jesus treated women that I understood how I, as a doctor, should treat them."

For the record, there is little to no scholarly evidence, even in the Apocrypha, that Jesus anally sodomized narcoleptic women in their sleep.

Unfortunately, Linda found herself in a trap familiar to women of powerful husbands. She had no savings of her own and little opportunity for making an income. So she suffered through a bad situation as long as she could.

"I would be asleep and since [the sodomy] was painful and threatening, I woke up," she said. "Sometimes I acquiesced once he had started, just to make it go faster, and sometimes I tried to push him off. . . . I would [confront] David later, and he would say, 'You asked me to do that,' and I would say, 'No, I never asked for it.'"

Linda also explained how Hager, in their fully conscious time together, would sometimes switch from vaginal to anal sex.

"He would say, 'Oh, I didn't mean to have anal sex with you; I can't feel the difference,'" Linda recalled her gynecologist husband saying. "And I would say, 'Well then, you're in the wrong business.'"

3.
The Loofah-Loving Splotchy-Headed Bloviator

Common Name:
Bill O'Reilly

Native Habitat:
The No-Spin Zone

Distinctive Appearance:
Splotchy exterior;
dark, rotten core

Natural Enemies:
Anyone who
documents his
words

To get a fair sense of just how big the October 2004 Bill O'Reilly/Andrea Mackris sexual harassment scandal really was, one need only do a simple Google search.

For instance, as of this writing, a search of "falafel" and "O'Reilly" produces 96,400 hits, whereas a search of "falafel" and "chickpea," the popular Middle Eastern dish's main ingredient, yields just 78,200 hits.

But as the authors of this book pointed out in their previous offering *Sweet Jesus, I Hate Bill O'Reilly,* Bill's sexual perversions run wide, deep, and most likely well into the eleven spatial and temporal dimensions predicted by string theory.

On his show, *The O'Reilly Factor,* Bill has run stories about sex parties on college campuses, porn stars, and Internet webcam performers. He even did one segment about a drive-thru coffee shop where girls in bikinis serve lattes. These stories are usually sandwiched between segments on child predators and rants about how major public figures are too afraid to come on his program.

They're also invariably accompanied by either video or an interview with the buxom women in question.

The frequency of these segments was quickly rising to absurd levels when, on February 1, 2007, conservative radio host Laura Ingraham visited *The Factor*. She took O'Reilly to task for the amount of T&A O'Reilly had been showing on the program. Of course, feminist that he is, Bill treated the whole thing as a joke. To add insult to injury, as Ingraham spoke, he ran video of a large-breasted woman, which looked more like an excerpt from a soft-core porno than a news clip.

O'Reilly announced, "We ran this last night for cosmetic surgery." Ingraham questioned the necessity of endlessly looping such videos and then brought up a *Factor* story about a nude party at an Ivy League school. O'Reilly responded, "Student activity fees were being used to fuel an orgy!" thus implying that it was in some way "news."

Igraham wasn't buying it.

Ingraham: You don't think people know what a nude party would look like?

O'Reilly: I don't think so.

Ingraham: Do they have to see it?

O'Reilly: I had to. I didn't know.

Yes, one could imagine that O'Reilly reviewed that video many times before it went to air. Probably with the office door closed, the "Do not disturb, under penalty of termination" sign displayed, and a fresh bottle of Astroglide handy.

Finally, in a moment of desperation, O'Reilly exclaimed, "I didn't shoot those shots!" This, of course, is a brilliant rejoinder—and somewhat akin to blaming Leni Riefenstahl for the Holocaust. Yes, Bill didn't actually film the bouncing boobies—he just reviewed them, saw them through editing, selected final length, and authorized their display on his nationally televised, highly rated political affairs program. He obviously had nothing to do with it!

But that weird disavowal actually segues nicely into the split in Bill's personality that careful observers of the man have observed for years. The frontman is a fighter for "traditional America." The guy behind the scenes is just a dirty old man. And sometimes those two dudes morph their protoplasm into a terrifying, freaky, sex-obsessed Moral-Puritan-Beast.

For instance, in his book *The O'Reilly Factor,* moral crusader Bill wrote at length and without perceptible irony about all the chicks who turned him on:

"For me, that means Tyra Banks in Victoria's Secret catalogs (can you believe you get these free?); Sarah Michelle Gellar in a tight T-shirt chasing a vampire or Jacqueline Bisset in a very wet T-shirt in *The Deep;* Vanessa Williams doing anything anywhere; Melanie Griffith before the lip implants and Sharon Stone reacting with such openness to Michael Douglas; Betty Grable in hot pants and Kim Basinger in no pants; Marilyn Monroe looking exhausted and the Spice Girls looking as if they know what they are singing (with the sound muted). And I'm talking about the full range from Mouseketeer Annette Funicello, when I was ten years old, to Connie Chung reading the news today (call me crazy, but she can tell me about Kosovo anytime)."

Oh, but it gets better.

Following are excerpts from the Andrea Mackris sexual harassment lawsuit complaint. Most of this stuff is available in *Sweet Jesus, I Hate Bill O'Reilly*—and the entire document is posted on thesmokinggun.com, which has referred to the action as "the greatest lawsuit ever."

During the course of this dinner, in approximately May 2003, Defendant BILL O'REILLY, without solicitation or invite, regaled Plaintiff and her friend with stories concerning the loss of his virginity to a girl in a car at JFK, two "really wild" Scandinavian airline stewardesses he had gotten together with, and a "girl" at a sex show in Thailand who had shown him things in a backroom that "blew [his] mind." Defendant then stated he was going to Italy to meet the Pope, that his pregnant wife was staying at home with his daughter, and implied he was looking forward to some extra-marital dalliances with the "hot" Italian women.

Yeah, that's entertainment all right. But here's the money shot:

> During the course of his monologue, Defendant O'REILLY further stated:
>
> "Well, if I took you down there then I'd want to take a shower with you right away, that would be the first [thing] I'd do . . . yeah, we'd check into the room, and we would order up some room service and uh and you'd definitely get two wines into you as quickly as I could get into you I would get 'em into you . . . maybe intravenously, get those glasses of wine into you . . .
>
> "You would basically be in the shower and then I would come in and I'd join you and you would have your back to me and I would take that little loofa thing and kinda' soap up your back . . . rub it all over you, get you to relax, hot water . . . and um . . . you know, you'd feel the tension drain out of you and uh you still would be with your back to me then I would kinda' put my arm—it's one of those mitts, those loofa mitts you know, so I got my hands in it . . . and I would put it around front, kinda' rub your tummy a little bit with it, and then with my other hand I would start to massage your boobs, get your nipples really hard . . . 'cuz I like that and you have really spectacular boobs . . .
>
> "So anyway I'd be rubbing your big boobs and getting your nipples really hard, kinda' kissing your neck from behind . . . and then I would take the other hand with the falafel [sic] thing and I'd put it on your pussy but you'd have to do it really light, just kind of a tease business."

Yeah. Ninety-six thousand hits. Seems kind of low, actually, when you think about it.

Of course, after this colossal public pantsing, Bill was more defiant than ever. Without really refuting any of Mackris's claims, he tried to set himself up as some kind of victim.

"Fame makes you a target," he said, as if to say that the accusations were baseless—without really saying it.

"I've received many threats over the years. Everything from death letters to some guy running around the country offering people $25,000 to sign affidavits accusing me of whatever."

Many of you are probably rightly asking, "What does this have to do with rubbing lunch on an employee's vagina?" The answer, of course, is nothing.

"It's a shame we have to live in a country where this happens, but got to go through it. All right, that's it. End of story."

After a rumored multimillion-dollar settlement, O'Reilly exclaimed, "The good news is that *Factor* viewers and listeners seemed to have given me the benefit of the doubt when some of the media did not. You guys looked out for me, and I will never forget it. This brutal ordeal is now officially over and I will never speak of it again."

That certainly doesn't mean, of course, that you shouldn't.

4.

The Illegal-Porn-Scouting Smith

Common Name:
Douglas Smith

Natural Habitat:
Wilderness; World
Wide Web

Distinctive Behaviors:
Scouting;
being unprepared

Contrary to decades of schoolyard bully rhetoric and everything science purports to know about males who wear neckerchiefs and spend long weekends frolicking out-of-doors in short pants with other males, if you're a member of the Boy Scouts of America, you're not necessarily gay.

In fact, if you want to be a member in good standing, you can't be. The Boy Scouts' official position is that homosexuality (as well as atheism and agnosticism) is contrary to the values of the Scout Oath and Law, and so the gayest activity on God's green earth outside of a *Mommie Dearest* party at Charles Nelson Reilly's is officially and until further notice closed to gays.

(In the interests of full disclosure, one of this book's coauthors—the nongay one, though you wouldn't know it from the pictures of him in his uniform at the Jamboree—was a Scout for several years back in the '70s. He wasn't happy about it, and in fact has confessed several times that if he'd been aware of the Scouts' discriminatory policies at the time, he'd have pulled his Scoutmaster aside on day one, cupped the gruff but avuncular mentor's hands in his own, and said, "You know, I don't believe in God, but if I did, I'd thank Him for those beautiful blue eyes of yours.")

Not surprisingly, there are a couple schools of thought on the whole gay Scout issue. Some believe that gay men lead inherently deviant lifestyles and are just out to have sex with anything sportin' external genitalia. And others think they're not deviant per se, but believe you wouldn't have a gay man watch over a bunch of prepubescent boys any more than you'd want a straight man be a Girl Scout troop leader. (On the other hand, one could make a strong argument that gay men would make totally awesome Girl Scout leaders in the tradition of Shelley Long's character, Phyllis Nefler, in *Troop Beverly Hills*.)

So the Boy Scouts have consistently reaffirmed a policy of grooming leaders who reflect the organization's values by being upright, God-fearing men who love women—though not in the way Isaac Mizrahi loves women.

Douglas Sovereign Smith knew this better than most. He had tons of Scouting experience at every level. He was a Scout as a boy and grew up loving the organization. And he would turn out to be everything a good Scout was supposed to be. He married and fathered two children. From 1978 to 1983, he headed the Thatcher Woods Area Boy Scout Council in Oak Park, Illinois. He continued to work for the Scouts for 39 years, largely in administrative positions and later as director of programming. Most significantly, he took over the highly respected Youth Protection Task Force, which worked to guard kids from sexual abuse. In 2002, Doug proudly wrote, "The Boy Scouts of America is a leader in the field of youth protection."

Three years later, in Germany, authorities were investigating a suspected child-porn trafficker. During a sting operation, they turned up Smith's e-mail address and contacted U.S. authorities.

According to published reports, Smith told authorities that he started downloading the child porn "by accident."

Now, anyone who has browsed the Web for any length of time

knows it's possible to accidentally come across pornography. But it's hard to believe one could simply stumble upon *child* pornography. Maybe if you were multitasking and accidentally typed, say, "Nickelodeon Kids' Choice Awards" and "fellatio" in your Google toolbar.

Still, this was a grave charge, and authorities needed to be certain that this wasn't just some giant mistake.

When police checked Smith's home computer, they found 520 images and video clips of child porn. As the *Chicago Sun-Times* noted, some of these images included "children engaging in sex acts."

On March 30, 2005, Smith pled guilty to possession and distribution of child pornography.

So what have we all learned from Doug? Well, we learned that just because a man is married to a woman, has children of his own, and works for a respected and venerable youth organization, it doesn't mean he's not a sick fucking bastard.

And, just as importantly, we learned that if you're surfing the Net and you "accidentally" download a few hundred pictures and videos of young children being forced into sexual situations, you should erase them. Then you should unplug your computer, take it outside, smash it on the lawn, and use the pieces to scoop out the parts of your cerebral cortex that retain any memory of the last, say, thirty years of your life.

5.

The Genital-Boasting Virginia GOPer

Common Name:
Robin Vanderwall

Native Habitat:
Republican circles

Mating Habits:
Particular interest in
13-year-olds

By November 2004, reality shows were already going downhill fast. The American public had been subjected to such tedious fare as *Married by America, Are You Hot?,* and *I'm a Celebrity, Get Me Out of Here,* just to name a few.

But the genre found new life when NBC had the brilliant idea of combining the surreal drama of *The Osbournes,* the sexual tension of *Temptation Island,* and the cheeky antics of *Kids Say the Darndest Things.* And thus was born *Dateline: To Catch a Predator.*

For the next few years, the American public would be asking themselves, "What are those crazy would-be pedophiles going to do next?" "How many sex perverts can there possibly be in Greenville, Ohio?" "Where will the pedophile auditions be held next week, and how many will go through to the next round?" and "Why do the producers always tell them to bring Mike's Hard Lemonade?"

Unfortunately, this popular series of cautionary tales came a year too late for Robin Vanderwall, a Regent University law student who had run several local Republican campaigns.

In addition to chatting online, Vanderwall filled his time with work for various conservative causes. He was being recruited to run the new Faith and Family Alliance, which, according to Vanderwall, was planning on taking "an active role in the upcoming Bush campaign." He had worked on the campaign of Robert F. McDonnell, a Virginia Beach Republican. (McDonnell became famous statewide when he claimed having anal or oral sex might disqualify a person from being a judge because they violate state law.)

Yes, Robin Vanderwall was only 34, but he had his roots firmly planted in the hallowed ground of conservative politics. He was another point of light for the redoubtable GOP.

Oh, but there had to be a catch. You see, Robin Vanderwall really, really wanted to have sex with 13-year-olds. It didn't matter if they were boys or girls—he just liked 'em young.

And in a rare instance of kismet, it just so happened that when Virginia Beach police set up a special unit to patrol chat rooms for predators, officers posed as 13-year-old boys and girls.

The *Virginian-Pilot* reported that during a period from November 2002 to January 2003, three officers posing as teens had chats with Vanderwall. The conversations all started innocently enough, but Vanderwall always pushed them to be more sexual. For instance, he asked the teens to meet him and offered to introduce them to "real" sex. And while one might argue that he was simply offering a tutorial on avoiding anal and oral sex to protect their future viability as Virginia judges, he would also brag about his genitals.

After arranging to meet Vanderwall, police arrested him. In July 2004, he was sentenced to seven years in prison for soliciting sex with minors.

Still, no one is beyond the reach of God's grace, and Vanderwall's attitudes toward the Web certainly changed during this experience. During one interview he said, "That thing is from Satan, as far as I'm concerned."

Fine. But as a former young up-and-comer in the GOP, Vanderwall might do well to heed the wisdom of his elders: The Internets and the Google don't attempt to molest 13-year-olds; Republican pedophiles attempt to molest 13-year-olds.

6.

The Alleged Catholic Co-Ed Rover

Common Name:
Deal Hudson

Natural Habitats:
White House;
academia

Natural Enemies:
Catholic newspapers;
freshman chicks

George W. Bush can really spot 'em. He's like a woman who keeps dating abusive men. He can't stop repeating the same pattern.

You'd have thought he was safe with Deal Hudson. The man was publisher of the conservative Catholic publication *Crisis,* for Christ's sake.

In 1998, he published a study concluding that Republicans could garner favor with traditionally Democratic Catholic voters by focusing their efforts on those who regularly attend Mass.

The piece caught the attention of Karl Rove, and Hudson joined the Bush campaign as an adviser.

Now, Deal wasn't just any adviser. After the 2000 election, he became a crucial link between the Bushies and Catholics.

Hudson was so important to the Bush camp that Catholic League president William Donohue, a boisterous true believer who often appears on television looking like he'd kick Mother Angelica's ass across St. Peter's Square if she ever confused *homoousios* with *homoiousios* while discussing the Nicene

Creed, said Hudson "had become the point man" and claimed "if you wanted to get something to the top inner circles of the White House from the Catholic perspective, you could contact Deal Hudson and it was delivered."

In *The Architect: Karl Rove and the Master Plan for Absolute Power*, authors James Moore and Wayne Slater referred to Hudson as the "right-hand man for Catholic outreach in the 2000 presidential campaign." So as the 2004 election approached, Hudson was a key member of the team.

But by August of 2004, their boundless mutual fetus adoration was not enough to keep the Bush-Hudson marriage together.

Hudson announced he was resigning from the Bush team over an investigation by a Catholic newspaper—believed to be *The National Catholic Reporter*, according to a report in the *New York Times*—into sexual harassment accusations that had been made years earlier.

From 1989 to 1995, Hudson taught at New York's Fordham University, perhaps best known as the school where Vince Lombardi roamed the gridiron as a member of the legendary Seven Blocks of Granite, but soon to become not quite as famous as the place where a future Bush campaign adviser would alledgedly spring a woody over a freshman chick.

Yes, instead of approaching his wife for a private vicar-and-tart party, Hudson did the Christian thing and found a drunk girl in a bar.

What he actually found was that the old cliché about Catholic schoolgirls isn't necessarily true. Turned out Deal could not close, and the woman, a freshman at the university, charged him with sexual harassment. Hudson resigned.

When the story of the newspaper investigation broke, Hudson played the victim. In a column for the online edition of the *National Review*, he claimed he was being subjected to "personal attacks" because of his support for Bush.

A little tip for Hudson, *O'Reilly Factor* viewers, and all the rest: If you sexually harass someone, proceed to portray yourself as an arbiter of morality, and then get busted for it, that's not a personal attack. It's what's known as "being held accountable for your actions" or "absolutely fucking hilarious."

In a book published in the year before the scandal broke, Hudson had talked about his mistakes, writing, "I experienced, the hard way, that passion does subside, and I was foolish not to realize that the love that follows is better."

Yes, the unconditional love intrinsic to a divinely ordained Catholic marriage is similar to *agape,* God's selfless love for humanity, and is widely considered, according to longstanding Catholic tradition, to be worth at least as much if not more than *five* drunk college freshman girls.

7.

The Incredibly Benevolent Sugar Daddy

Common Name:
Richard Dasen

Native Habitat:
Christian Financial
Counseling office;
motel rooms

Distinctive Behaviors:
Christian charity;
promotion
of prostitution

"Until he was arrested this year in his underwear in a motel room with a nearly naked young woman who was behind in her payments to his finance company, no businessman in this town was more respected than Richard A. Dasen Sr."

If you ever wanted to write the great American novel, that would be as good an opening as any.

Unfortunately, you'd first have to get permission from the *Washington Post,* because they wrote it first. For as compelling a character as Richard Dasen might have been in fiction, unhappily for all those around him, he is quite real.

On the surface, Dasen was a do-gooder. As recounted in a 2004 *Washington Post* profile (from which the above excerpt was lifted), he led local building projects in the Kalispell, Montana, area that improved his community. He also served as an elder in his church and helped people manage their finances through a nonprofit outfit called Christian Financial Counseling.

But his philanthropic activities were hardly limited to volunteer work. It wasn't uncommon to see checks for $1,000, $2,000, or even $5,000 given to women who had found themselves in need. Unfortunately, it turned out that the women on the receiving end of his generosity also invariably found themselves on the receiving end of his boner.

Apparently, Dasen was using Christian Financial Counseling as his own private whorehouse. Problem was, the women weren't actually whores until he got hold of them.

As the *Washington Post* reported: "Many of the women Dasen allegedly paid for sex met him when they came to Christian Financial Counseling for help in consolidating and managing their debts. Dasen ran the nonprofit organization and also owns a private finance firm, Budget Finance.

"Detectives have interviewed about 40 of these women, and many of them have said that Dasen 'used their indebtedness to him to coerce them to have sex,' Kalispell Police Chief Frank Garner said."

Now, Dasen was not just another sorry bastard who succumbed to the devil's charms. No, he was clearly Satan himself. According to testimony in court documents, if Dasen was not completely satisfied with sexual services rendered, he would often "arrange for repossession of vehicles that he . . . purchased or funded for those females, through his finance company." Talk about pressure to perform.

Sadly, an apparent side effect of Dasen's Christian charity was a rise in the fortunes of local drug dealers. According to Charles Harball, Kalispell's city attorney, Dasen single-handedly funded the area methamphetamine trade as women who were hooked on the drug began to see him as a ready source of cash. Indeed, after he was arrested there was a "flood of petty crime from addicts seeking cash for their habit," said Harball.

In May of 2005, Dasen was convicted of promotion of prostitution, sexual abuse of children, and four counts of prostitution. He was sentenced to two years in prison.

In December of 2005, a jury awarded a teenage girl more than

$2 million in damages after Dasen allegedly forced the girl and a friend, aged 16 and 15, to perform sex acts for money.

Now, somehow this is all hard to square with the profile of a man who one local activist had called "incredibly benevolent" and a backer of conservative Christian causes. Even Solomon, whom the Bible claimed had 700 wives and 300 concubines, would have no doubt avoided such an unflattering portrait as the following:

"When Dasen talked to police shortly after his arrest, he characterized his for-pay sexual activities with young women as 'helping' them, according to a detective's affidavit that summarizes Dasen's conversation with police," wrote the *Post* in their August 2004 profile of Dasen. "When a detective asked him to explain how he was helping the women, the affidavit said that Dasen replied that when he thought about it, he realized he was not helping them after all.

"Dasen said, too, that he believes he has a problem, perhaps an addiction. But he added, according to the affidavit, that he believes he is more addicted to 'helping' than to sex."

Alas, dear Richard, we all have our crosses to bear.

8.

The Kid-Flashing Texas Rush Wannabe

Common Name:
Jon Matthews

Distinctive Behaviors:
Bashing liberals;
using extremely
poor judgment

Status:
In captivity

When you're a right-winger in Texas, you're bona fide.

These are the kinds of guys who might have listened to an economics lecture from Jude Wanniski, agreed with it in principle, and then beat the shit out of him for having a queer-sounding name and wearing one of them faggy ties.

If you're from Houston, your conservatism is likely even more distilled. After all, this is the home of George Bush Intercontinental Airport, Halliburton, and the nation's only perfect 1:1 ratio of sexually suggestive novelty mudflaps to testicles.

So if you're a right-wing Houston radio talk show host, well, chances are that deep down you probably think Ronald Reagan was a socialist and G. Gordon Liddy is a fag.

And the chance of your eventually pleading guilty to exposing yourself to an 11-year-old girl? Oh, let's just say that's got to be pretty close to 100 percent.

From the mid-'80s to the early 2000s, Jon Matthews was a well-known character in

Houston radio. A reliable critic of Bill Clinton and liberals in general, he also wrote a local newspaper column, becoming the target of a libel suit after referring to the Sugar Land, Texas, mayor as "Mayor Osama."

But just like his pill-poppin' colleague Rush Limbaugh, Jon Matthews had a little secret.

On October 9, 2003, Matthews' young neighbor girl came over to play with a puppy. It was a charming Norman Rockwell moment that Matthews appeared determined to turn into a hellish Hieronymus Bosch nightmare.

When he answered the door, Matthews was standing there in his underwear. And according to court documents, the girl claimed that when he sat down on the floor his genitals were exposed.

Now most adults know that when the neighbor kids stop by for a visit, you put some clothes on. Let's just call it a rule. And, indeed, it looked like one of those social niceties Matthews himself was going to follow after he left the room and put on a pair of shorts.

However, according to court documents, "upon his return to the living room, the defendant pulled his shorts and underwear down and exposed his genitals" to the girl and said "whoops." He then told her not to tell anyone what he had done.

After later receiving seven years' probation stemming from a June 2004 plea agreement, Matthews released this statement:

"Those of you who have listened to my radio show and read my newspaper columns over the years know how strong a supporter I was of our criminal justice system. I can only say how misguided I was. Our criminal justice system is not based on justice; it is a quota system where conviction is the only scorecard."

So at this point in the game, the scorecard read: Justice system 1, Jon Matthews 0, number of nightmares you will now be forced to endure involving a puppy, a pair of loose-fitting shorts, and Jon Matthews's balls, 72.

Oh, but there was more to come.

In August of 2006, Matthews was back in court for allegedly

violating his probation. He had been accused of abusing alcohol and was kicked out of a sex offenders' counseling program for alleged inappropriate online sexual conduct.

Now, while most people can go a few years without, as the *Houston Chronicle* described the allegations, "viewing obscene material over the Internet" or participating in an "Internet fantasy message exchange" in which one describes "sex acts performed on a 3-year-old boy," it's apparently a struggle for a surprisingly large percentage of right-wing Houston talk show hosts.

As the local Community Supervision and Corrections Department reported, "Mr. Matthews presented himself to be a female stripper who took her three-year-old son to work with her. The defendant described sexual acts between the strippers and the three-year-old boy."

And from the thank-goodness-for-small-favors hall of fame, the *Houston Chronicle,* after quoting the above report, noted that Matthews did not in fact have a 3-year-old son.

In February, a judge revoked his probation and ordered him to serve three years in prison.

Somehow, it's hard to escape the feeling that if an Air America Radio host were caught up in this sort of thing, it would be the subject of wall-to-wall coverage on Fox News and at least three *Hannity on America* specials.

Guess how much airtime Fox gave *this* story?

Good guess.

9.

The Clinton-Bashing, Alleged Child-Predator Glickman

Common Name:
Marty Glickman

Distinctive Call:
"We remain
outraged"

Mating Habits:
Allegedly plying
young girls with
LSD

Current Habitat:
In the boneyard

Composer Philip Glass wrote three "portrait" operas between 1975 and 1984: *Einstein on the Beach, Satyagraha,* and *Akhnaten.*

The trilogy explored three great men, including a revolutionary scientist, an icon of peace, and the first monotheistic pharaoh of Egypt. If Mr. Glass were to create a fourth portrait opera, he might want to consider Marty Glickman.

As a rule of thumb, operas aren't funny. Now, some of you with season tickets to the Met might say, "Well, what about the *Barber of Seville? Cosi fan tutte? Die Fledermaus? Ariadne auf Naxos? Gianni Schicchi? . . .*" Okay, okay, okay, *most* operas aren't funny. They just aren't. So don't expect this one to be any different.

Act I

It is March 1999. The president of the United States has admitted to an affair with a young White House intern. He has lied to the nation. Now the great Democratic president who was so despised by a small faction of conservative America is wounded and the sharks are circling.

Marty Glickman, a popular Florida political commentator who often guest-hosted on local radio and was known affectionately as "Republican Marty," is incensed.

The young woman at the center of the scandal is giving her first television interview as America watches.

The following day, Marty Glickman stands in front of Tallahassee's Old Capitol amid supporters. On this day he poses beside a portrait of President Clinton holding a baseball bat. He swings it with the force and fury of Thor's legendary warhammer and destroys the picture.

Libretto: "We want to send a message from this community that even though the impeachment trial is over, we remain outraged. We think the president of the United States ought to be above reproach. Let's get someone in there that little children do not have to whisper about in each other's ears."

Protesters hold banners reading, "Honk if you believe Clinton is a rapist" and other pearls of political discourse.

As the scene closes, Glickman proclaims that he wants to debate the president: "I'm serious. I want him to quit hiding behind his wife's skirt and address that question. I'm not going to go away until I get an answer."

Act II

It is April 2001.

Marty Glickman is released from Florida's Leon County Jail. He faces charges that could bring a lengthy prison term. Like his arch-nemesis, Bill Clinton, Republican Marty is caught up in a sex scandal. Unlike Clinton, the girls Glickman was connected to were underage and allegedly plied with cash and LSD.

The stage is bare. There are no signs or shattered portraits. Just an eerie silence.

Act III

It is May 2001.

Three weeks after his arrest, Marty Glickman is at home, released on bail. He sees his life before him. He sees his past. Does he see hypocrisy? The audience can only guess.

Following an aria worthy of *Aida,* Glickman swallows an undisclosed substance, cuts his wrists, and stabs himself in the chest.

The wounds are superficial, but he eventually dies from the poison.

As the stage darkens, we see Glickman's sister sobbing: "I want the public to know that Marty was not a drug dealer and didn't do drugs."

"He was set up by a couple of bad little girls."

Fin.

10.

The Great Masturbating Southeastern Glavin

Common Name:
Matthew Glavin

Distinctive Behaviors:
Heading a conservative legal foundation that sought to disbar President Clinton, contested affirmative-action policies, and fought to keep gays from becoming scoutmasters; whacking off in the park

Habitat:
The park

Do you like to masturbate? Sure, we all do. It's easy and fun, and a great way to pass the time. But as with all good things, there's a time and a place.

Matthew Glavin was president and CEO of the conservative Southeastern Legal Foundation. The organization fought against affirmative-action policies and same-sex partner benefits. It pushed for President Clinton to be disbarred. It aided the Boy Scouts in their fight to keep gays from being scoutmasters. And its leader had absolutely no clue where it was appropriate to rub his wiener.

Glavin was living in Alpharetta, Georgia, on May 17, 2000, when he decided to take a stroll through the Chattahoochee River National Recreation Area. While walking along a trail near the river, he ran into a man named Brett Morris. Although he didn't know Morris, he struck up a conversation. So far, so good. The conversation took a curious and irrevocable turn, however, when Glavin started masturbating through his shorts.

Now, certainly different cultures have

varying standards for what constitutes personal space, but this is considered a little too informal no matter where you are.

But then Glavin decided to take it up a notch and, according to Morris, reached over to fondle Morris's groin.

So here we come to a fork in the narrative where one can imagine two possible outcomes. Brett could have gotten a big smile on his face, responded in kind, and the two might have lived happily ever after . . . or at least had a memorable couple of hours. Or he might have recoiled in horror, coming away none too happy about being groped on public land by a closeted freak. You see where this is going.

Well, it turned out that Brett Morris was actually an undercover U.S. Park Service officer from the Medlock Bridge area. The region had apparently become the Studio 54 of local public parklands and the Park Service was trying to get a handle on the situation. And while Morris was certainly looking for lewd behavior, he didn't necessarily expect to become the object of a cup-and-squeeze.

Glavin resigned from the Southeastern Legal Foundation, where he had served since 1994. He denied the pending charge and claimed that his resignation was "to protect my family and the foundation."

In December, he was sentenced to a year of probation on charges of public indecency, and was ordered to stay out of federal parks during that time.

Curiously, Glavin had apparently done this before. He received probation and a park ban back in 1996 on a similar charge.

It's difficult to say which is more disturbing—that a closeted, self-loathing gay guy was heading up one of the leading conservative organizations in the country, or that he was apparently a moron as well. Why doesn't he just stay out of parks?!

If only this had happened later in his life, Glavin could have learned from the immortal words of George W. Bush: "Fool me once . . . shame on . . . shame on you. Fool me . . . you can't get fooled again."

DIDJAKNOW?

Former federal judge G. Harrold Carswell, a Nixon Supreme Court nominee who was rejected by the Senate in 1970 was charged with battery and "attempting to commit an unnatural and lascivious act" in connection with a June 1976 incident involving a male undercover officer.

11.
The Midwestern Anti-Gay-Adoption Kimmerling

Common Name:
Earl Kimmerling

Native Habitat:
Indiana

Distinctive Behaviors:
Saving kids
from gay adoption,
then molesting them

Nothing inflames the fertile gonads of a fundamentalist Christian quite like the issue of gay adoption. Why? Well, it's not altogether clear.

The myth that two men aren't capable of raising a child together was thoroughly debunked by the late-'80s NBC sitcom *My Two Dads*.

This pre-DNA-testing case study focused on a girl who was being raised by two men, either of whom might have knocked up her dearly departed, apparently slutty mom.

Now, the heads of this TV household were both obviously heterosexual. And that could be why the religious right didn't take all that much offense. And in case there was any question as to the fully patriarchal nature of this nontraditional family, Dick Butkus was cast as the manly manager of the café in their apartment building. Got it? They were all straight.

Unfortunately, in real life, the waters invariably become muddied whenever two dads share more than the fruits of their mutual girlfriend's loins.

And so it was for Craig Peterson.

The suburban Indianapolis man was everything the religious right feared and hated: a gay man who wanted to be a father.

Now, he could have easily found a surrogate and brought a biological child or two into the world. But no, he selfishly decided to pursue the adoption of three brothers and a sister from the foster care system, all of whom were victims of fetal alcohol syndrome. The bastard!

Peterson, who was single, immersed himself in research, learning how to deal with the children's disabilities and finding appropriate schools. Eventually, the local adoption board unanimously agreed to place the four children with him. So it was shaping up as one of those idyllic, made-for-*Oprah* stories about the limitless potential of unconditional love.

Or so it was until the girl's foster parents, Earl "Butch" and Saundra Kimmerling, found out that Peterson was gay.

Suddenly, Peterson's fitness for raising a young girl was called into question, and the Kimmerlings were leading the charge. Oh, yes, imagine the long, grueling summers filled with nothing but Paris cafes, lavish Broadway shows, and shoe shopping. Why not just sell her organs now and spare her this life of unimaginable toil?

Soon, Butch was the Christian right's new flavor of the month as he flogged the case of the deprived little girl to anyone who would listen.

The couple's pastor sent letters to area churches asking them to oppose the adoption. Even their mayor came out to support their crusade.

And so inspired were Republican representatives Woody Burton and Jack Lutz that they sponsored a bill to prevent gays from adopting children.

In December of 1998, the Kimmerlings adopted the girl. Peterson went ahead with the adoption of the boys, who were placed with him earlier that year.

After the controversy over the little girl erupted, Peterson said, "The whole thing was just like a real odd movie. . . . Like a scary movie or something."

Well, that scary movie was about to enter its bloodcurdling third act.

Yes, like so many upstanding, antigay conservatives who are committed to protecting children, Earl Kimmerling had a secret. Just a year after adopting the little girl, this champion of traditional family values pleaded guilty to four counts of child molestation. Three guesses who the victim was.

Now, during the custody fight, the Kimmerlings wrote a letter to the *Indianapolis Star* outlining their concerns. It read, in part: "Girls need mothers so they can learn what it is to be a woman; they need fathers so they know how to interact with the opposite sex."

Well, our young heroine certainly got an education in all of that. Kimmerling is serving a 40-year sentence.

12.

The Green-and-Gold-Striped Self-Righteous Chmura

Common Name:
Mark Chmura

Natural Habitat:
Lambeau Field;
suburban Wisconsin
post-prom parties

Distinctive Behaviors:
Hot-tubbing;
president-snubbing

Status:
Roaming free

Former Green Bay Packer Mark Chmura was what you would call a good Christian. Indeed, he was the kind of good Christian who would eventually leave his wife at home while attending a high school post-prom party where he drank heavily before stripping down to his undershorts and getting in a hot tub with teenage girls.

You see, Chmura, a Pro Bowl tight end and big GOP booster, referred to the Bible as his "playbook for life." Unfortunately, when he should have run a post route to the glory and grace of the Lord Jesus Christ, he instead got himself accused of sexually assaulting his kids' 17-year-old babysitter at a party in a southeastern Wisconsin home.

Now, it's important to point out that Chmura was ultimately acquitted of the crime. So in the eyes of the law he didn't do anything wrong.

But this party wasn't exactly the wedding at Cana either. More like the post-prom hot tub party at Cana featuring the miracle of the wine and the watery underpants.

Indeed, after his acquittal Chmura was somewhat more chastened than righteous, admitting that his behavior at the party "wasn't something a married man should do."

Even so, the jurors who heard the case were somewhat less forgiving.

"None of us believed nothing happened. We all believed something happened in there," one female juror who asked her name not be used told the AP. "But we had no evidence to prove it."

Jury foreman Brad Breidenstein also appeared to have his suspicions:

"We all agreed that they were in that bathroom together. But we don't really know what took place," Breidenstein told the AP.

After the verdict, Chmura cited the jury's decision as evidence that the God of the universe intercedes on behalf of wealthy professional athletes who get in legal trouble for carousing with teens at Milwaukee-area suburban hot tub parties.

"I thank my Lord and Savior Jesus Christ, my wife, and my legal team and my friends who supported me," said Chmura, at which point the Holy Spirit totally high-fived him.

After being acquitted, Chmura said he would be going to Disney World.

Yeah, that's actually not a joke.

Ironically enough, Chmura boycotted the Packers' White House visit after their 1997 Super Bowl victory because he didn't like President Clinton.

In 1998, after Clinton admitted to sexual contact with Monica Lewinsky, Chmura was not shy about criticizing the president:

"I look like a genius now," Chmura told the *Milwaukee Journal Sentinel*. "I kind of knew it all along. He just got caught in another lie and this one escalated.

"I'm just shocked at the nation and how they're still accepting the guy. It doesn't really say much for society and the morals he sets forth for our children. What's he saying, that it's OK to lie and do the things that he's done?"

Ah, but something didn't quite ring true to Wisconsin's no-nonsense populace. Their Spidey sense was tingling.

Shortly after the quote ran, columnist Andy Fenelon was deluged with a series of WTF? letters.

"How could you print that [expletive]," read one.

"What a [expletive] hypocrite," declared another.

"One day," another note said, "it will all come back to haunt him."

13.
The Press-Room-Dwelling, Ass-Peddling Guckert

Common Name:
Jeff Gannon

Native Habitat:
White House
briefing room;
hotmilitarystud.com

*Distinctive
Characteristics:*
Total top for clients;
total bottom for the
administration

When reporter Jeff Gannon was famously outed as a former gay escort and working Republican shill during the salad days of the Bush presidency—before the public's raw cynicism ultimately and inevitably yielded to pure Oedipal-eye-plucking horror—he explained, as was recounted in a February 2005 *Washington Post* story, that "he did not use a pseudonym to hide his past but because his real last name is hard to spell and pronounce."

Given that he came to fame as a frequently invited guest to White House press conferences, he might have helpfully explained who the morons were who were calling on him.

So was he burdened with a consonant-heavy Polish moniker, or a !Kung surname laden with a bewildering sequence of nearly indistinguishable vowels and clicks?

Almost. Jeff Gannon was born James Dale Guckert.

Of course, Gannon's new nom de plume must have felt right, as he and Guckert certainly seemed like different people.

Whereas Guckert advertised himself as a

$200-an-hour gay escort, Gannon wrote snide remarks about John Kerry's "pro-gay agenda" and sneered that gay activists' responses to Rick Santorum's famously antigay remarks were "predictable responses."

Of course, his gay-escort name, Bulldog, failed to hint at an ideology. But it was ironic in the extreme.

Indeed, it would be unfair to say that Gannon pitched the president softball questions. These were tee-balls, and the short-stop was a one-armed, asthmatic World of Warcraft addict with a paralyzing fear of grass.

Jeff Gannon first started covering the White House in February of 2003. At the time, he had little reporting experience and was not affiliated with any legitimate news organization.

He had, however, been affiliated with hotmilitarystud.com.

That wasn't a joke.

To be fair, before joining the press corps, Helen Thomas had appeared in no fewer than 14 pornographic "talkies" from 1939 to 1942.

That was a joke.

Now, the fact that a former male prostitute could gain access to White House briefings by using a bullshit name and credentials from a fake news organization—without the usual security vetting—is just insane. But it wasn't nearly as bizarre as what he did once he got inside.

On February 2, 2005, the liberal media watchdog group Media Matters noted "numerous instances" over the previous year where Gannon had asked comically softball questions of White House Press Secretary Scott McClellan.

They pointed out that the questions would "often include false assumptions favorable to the Bush administration." They also found that the questions consistently moved the conversation away from tough issues such as "the proposed Federal Marriage Amendment; the Bush administration's relationship with former Iraqi National Congress leader Ahmad Chalabi; the growing trade deficit with China; and President Bush's Texas Air National Guard record."

When reporters asked McClellan hard questions about the proposed Federal Marriage Amendment and growing trade deficits, we were treated to such pointed queries as:

"Doesn't Joe Wilson owe the president and America an apology for his deception and his own intelligence failure?"

"And doesn't that, combined with the now-proven al Qaeda link between Iraq—between Saddam Hussein and the terrorist organization—unequivocally make the case for going to war in Iraq?"

Had there been time for a follow-up, he almost certainly would have asked, "May I blow you? Please, sir, may I blow you?"

At another briefing, when reporters started drilling McClellan on possible threats to *Roe v. Wade,* Gannon face-planted McClellan with this:

"I'd like to comment on the angry mob that surrounded Karl Rove's house on Sunday. They chanted and pounded on the windows until the D.C. police and Secret Service were called in. The protest was organized by the National People's Action Coalition, whose members receive taxpayer funds, as well as financial support from groups including Teresa Heinz Kerry's Tides Foundation."

Was there a question in there? Oh, and for the record, it's not Teresa Heinz Kerry's Tides Foundation. It's the Tides Foundation.

But this was just coquettish eye-batting compared to the full-on reacharound he delivered during the controversy surrounding Bush's military record:

"Since there have been so many questions about what the president was doing over 30 years ago, what is it that he did after his honorable discharge from the National Guard? Did he make speeches alongside Jane Fonda, denouncing America's racist war in Vietnam? Did he testify before Congress that American troops committed war crimes in Vietnam? And did he throw somebody else's medals at the White House to protest a war America was still fighting? What was he doing after he was honorably discharged?"

A February 2005 editorial from the *San Francisco Chronicle* may have summed up the whole Gannon/Guckert affair best:

"It's hard to say which is worse: That the White House had no idea who it was allowing to be within shouting distance of the president—or that it knew exactly who Jeff Gannon was and why he was there."

With all due respect, the worst part is that a decorated military combat veteran was taking shit from a couple of knuckleheads whose own military service was limited to the Texas Air National Guard and hotmilitarystud.com.

14.
The Georgia Mule Dear

Common Name:
Neal Horsley

Distinctive Behaviors:
Animal husbandry

Distinctive Call:
"You peope are so
far removed from
the reality . . ."

Status:
Penitent

Sometimes these things come pretty close to just writing themselves. Case in point: Neal Horsley.

Horsley is an antiabortion activist and former webmaster of the notorious "Nuremberg Files," a site that listed the names and addresses of abortion doctors, which some claimed amounted to illegal intimidation. The site was vigorously challenged in the courts for its allegedly threatening nature, and a free-speech case involving the list nearly made it to the Supreme Court.

But while Horsley is undoubtedly best known for his passionate antiabortion advocacy, it's his passionate mule-fucking that earned him a place in this pantheon.

Yes, the man whose Web site includes (under the headline "Arresting Homosexuals [for their own good])," a warning to "homosexuals, or adulterers, or fornicators, or pedophiles, or beast fornicators and beast suckers" was apparently taking seriously the old writer's admonition to "write what you know."

In May of 2005, Horsley made a widely reported admission on Alan Colmes's radio show—in the process revealing Colmes for the effete, out-of-touch, pointy-headed New York liberal he really is:

Horsley: Hey, Alan, if you want to accuse me of having sex when I was a fool, I did everything that crossed my mind that looked like I . . .

Colmes: You had sex with animals?

Horsley: Absolutely. I was a fool. When you grow up on a farm in Georgia, your first girlfriend is a mule.

Colmes: I'm not so sure that that is so.

Horsley: You didn't grow up on a farm in Georgia, did you?

Colmes: Are you suggesting that everybody who grows up on a farm in Georgia has a mule as a girlfriend?

Horsley: It has historically been the case. You people are so far removed from the reality. . . . Welcome to domestic life on the farm. You experiment with anything that moves when you are growing up sexually. You're naive. You know better than that. . . . If it's warm and it's damp and it vibrates, you might in fact have sex with it.

15.

The Arizona Campaign-Managing, Minor-Corrupting Aiken

Common Name:
Stephen Aiken

Distinctive Behaviors:
Corruption of
minors

Mating Habits:
Not one to let
sleeping boobs lie

Hiring good staff is crucial to a successful political campaign. A bad hire who does something to embarrass a candidate can bring disaster in a media climate where minor squalls can quickly turn into major hurricanes.

Hell, it doesn't even have to be someone on the payroll. Tune in to Fox News on any given day and you're likely to hear "breaking news" about a supporter of a Democratic candidate—perhaps a random blogger or celebrity fundraiser attendee—who said something off-color in a venue that had nothing to do with said candidate.

The comment might be about Catholicism, or the war, or any other topic that hosts like Bill O'Reilly and Sean Hannity could use to inflame the dry underbrush of their viewers' minds.

Now, you yourself might say, "Hey! But one of those bloggers said Catholicism is for feebleminded ninnies . . . and I'm Catholic! And I myself happen to believe in the literal transubstantiation of crackers and fermented grapes into the body and blood of preindustrial Mediterranean woodworkers! So, thanks be to Fox News."

But while such tenuous associations should rightly be considered meager fodder for the punditry, those with more official ties to candidates do deserve scrutiny. Yet for some reason many of these stories go unnoticed by conservative radio and cable news.

Take the case of Stephen Aiken, the onetime campaign manager for Arizona Republican congressional candidate Randy Graf. Near the end of the 2006 midterm election cycle, it came out that Aiken had had some minor skirmishes with the law. While this story may not have had the resonance of a throwaway Rosie O'Donnell comment on *The View,* Aiken had, it turned out, been convicted in 1996 of "corruption of minors."

Apparently, Aiken had sexual contact with two girls he met through YouthQuest, a Christian counseling agency he worked with in Pennsylvania. According to the *Philadelphia Inquirer,* one victim said that Aiken "came into her room while she was asleep, undressed her and began to rub her breasts."

Aiken claims he was falsely convicted, and Graf, at least initially, appeared to back him up.

"What he did was no more serious than providing a teenager with beer," Graf told ABC News. "I believe Steve when he says he was falsely accused."

Really Randy? Hate to be the skunk at the party, but it's a *little* more serious. Still, next time you're thinking about running for Congress and you're riffling through a stack of resumes from potential campaign managers, you might want to put the ones from guys who've served jail time on sex charges in the B pile.

Of course, all this begs the question: Were there no other qualified candidates for the job? Was Graf deluged with applicants who couldn't get through a job interview without mentioning their bizarre Shetland pony fetish or their brief but unfulfilling stint as the Green River Killer?

But while Graf fired Aiken shortly after his conviction was made public, Aiken continued to hold his head up high.

At www.steveaiken.com (which, incidentally, looks like

something the rest of the Internet might have vomited into a pail), Aiken notes that he is available to speak at your "Church, Adult Bible study, Mens [*sic*] group or Civic organization." He'll dazzle you with such topics as "Current Events, Attacks on Christianity, Islamic Facsism [*sic*], Globalism, Immigration, and Bible Prophecy."

He also posts a series of "Steve's One-Liners." For instance, on the ACLU he writes, "They give me aggidda, trying to tear the pages of history out of this countries Christian Heritage, nothing but a bunch of hypocrytes!"

Oh, Randy Graf, you wily devil. While one can hardly condone your slick Machiavellian ways, you are owed a grudging measure of respect. Where oh where did you ever find this gem?

As proof of his conservative Republican bona fides, Aiken has also posted pictures of himself with party stalwarts such as George H. W. Bush, Bob Dole, John Ashcroft, Tom DeLay, Jerry Falwell, Gary Bauer, Ken Starr, and Ollie North—some of which, frankly, look not so much like photo opportunities as the last known picture of a suspected stalker.

In the "endorsements" section he includes a number of conservative anti–illegal immigration groups, a Bible-based women's organization, an anti-PETA group, and, of course, Daglio's Authentic Philadelphia Cheesesteaks and Hoagies.

But the most tantalizing tidbit on the site is the promo for his latest book. Come on, a far-right Christian conservative and Washington insider who parties with teens? It sounds like *American Pie* meets *Road Trip* meets *The Passion of the Christ*.

Well, probably more like Ambien meets Lunesta meets Rozerem.

Aiken notes that the book is "written from a Christian perspective" and promises to be "the story of my life with a self-help approach." And if you still haven't whipped that Visa out, it also covers the period from "breaking my neck to coming back later and winning a state racquetball championship." He then closes the sale with, "my wife and I hold nothing back in sharing the biblical life lessons we have learned."

Say what you want about liberals, but after their sex scandals at least they stay remotely interesting.

16.
The Republican Forcible Sodomizer of the Year

Common Name:
Mark Grethen

Distinguishing Features:
Generosity;
political awareness;
perversion

Status:
Convicted sex
offender; former
GOP award-winner
(status revoked)

Ours is a world awash in superlatives. In just about every human pursuit—entertainment, business, sales, art—new awards spring up daily like early morning dew.

Digesting this smorgasbord of huzzahs can, of course, be a chore. To hear that someone is an award-winning chef might simply mean their landmark work on the Target snack bar nachos combo has earned them employee of the month honors for April.

It's worse, of course, in the deeply superficial world of Washington politics, where tradition dictates that men who have received more penicillin shots than Bangkok be called "gentlemen" and our president hands out Medals of Freedom with the same discrimination that kindergarten teachers distribute gold stars for not peeing on the hamster.

So when Mark Grethen was invited to Washington to accept a Republican of the Year Award from the National Republican Congressional Committee's Business Advisory Council, well, it wasn't exactly Caesar Augustus' triumph through the streets of Rome.

But it was still an honor, and one the Suffolk, Virginia, man might have gladly accepted under normal circumstances. But there was a problem.

You see, Mark wasn't perfect. And like many other good, well-meaning, salt-of-the-earth people, he had made a few mistakes. Some folks take that home-office deduction when it's really more of a game room. Some hire an illegal alien to tend to the lawn, knowing full well they probably shouldn't. And Mark Grethen, that model conservative and generous donor to the NRCC, forcibly sodomized children.

Yes, while 2000, when he made his last donation to the NRCC, was no doubt a banner year for Grethen, it was 2001, when he was convicted of six sex crimes involving children, that really shone through.

Unfortunately, Grethen had been selected for the award through the organization's donor history, which the group apparently forgot to cross-reference with the state's sex-offender registry. Nor had the NRCC noticed that Grethen's last known address was the Deep Meadow Correctional Center.

Of course, when they found out, they took back the award, which was probably pretty easy as, let's face it, this wasn't exactly like stripping a novelist of his Nobel Prize. More like refusing to sell a World's Greatest Grandpa mug to a guy at the Circle K.

"We weren't aware of his current predicament. Otherwise, [the invitation] never would have been extended," NRCC spokesman Carl Forti told the Associated Press.

Well, duh.

Three Books and a Porno: Conservatives and Their Art

It seems that hardly an election cycle goes by without some prominent conservative wringing his hands over the liberal plot to replace the Western canon with a series of radical-feminist-penned graphic novels about armies of foulmouthed gay aboriginal Jesuses roaming the countryside in leather-daddy outfits fighting evil lesbian nuns and apocalyptic fetus-devouring Presbyterians under the direction of a meth-dealing Pat Robertson and his brown-skinned catamite sidekick, Pepe.

At best, such criticisms are exaggerated.

But when conservatives aren't busy condemning dirty novels and Hollywood filth, many can be found happily producing it.

Indeed, there exist at least three sex-soaked conservative-authored books and one failed Republican-financed adult film project that thoroughly strain the bounds of irony, if not the cash registers at Barnes & Noble.

Following is a summary of each:

LYNNE CHENEY'S Sisters

Moral crusader, Second Lady, and renowned future-lesbian-incubator Lynne Cheney once headed the National Endowment for the Humanities. In 1995, she founded the American Council of Trustees and Alumni, an organization "committed to academic freedom, excellence and accountability at America's colleges and universities."

Clearly, the ACTA's first order of business should have been keeping Lynne's breathless lesbian novel *Sisters* out of college English literature curricula lest it midwife even more openly gay relatives for the Cheney family to go apoplectic over.

Yes, in 1981, Mrs. Cheney wrote the lesbian-themed Western, which is now so hard to get that copies have sold for as much as $600.00 on Amazon.com (plus $3.99 for shipping). By contrast, as of this writing, her 1996 screed against relativism, *Telling the Truth*, can be had for the low, low price of US$.01.

Luckily though, several Web-savvy fans of conservative Republican homoeroticism have helpfully posted excerpts from the former.

Enjoy:

"The women who embraced in the wagon were Adam and Eve crossing a dark cathedral stage—no, Eve and Eve, loving one another as they would not be able to once they ate of the fruit and knew themselves as they truly were. She felt curiously moved, curiously envious of them. She had never to this moment thought Eden a particularly attractive paradise, based as it was on naivete, but she saw that the women in the cart had a passionate, loving intimacy forever closed to her. How strong it made them. What comfort it gave."

"The note was short. 'Helen, my joy and my beloved,'

It began: 'Why do we stay? I have no reason beyond a few pupils who would miss me briefly, and your life would be infinitely better away from him. Let us go away together, away from the anger and imperatives of men. We shall find ourselves a secluded bower where they dare not venture. There will be only the two of us, and we shall linger through long afternoons of sweet retirement. In the evenings I shall read to you while you work your cross-stitch in the firelight. And then we shall go to bed, our bed, my dearest girl. . . .'"

Lewis Libby's The Apprentice

In 1996, I. Lewis "Scooter" Libby, the disgraced former chief of staff to Vice President Dick Cheney, wrote a novel about the goings-on at a remote Japanese inn. In 2005, the novel was resurrected by Lauren Collins in *The New Yorker.*

Thankfully, Collins took the bullet for all of us, culling some of the juicier bits for her piece. Wrote Collins:

"One passage goes, 'At length he walked around to the deer's head and, reaching into his pants, struggled for a moment and then pulled out his penis. He began to piss in the snow just in front of the deer's nostrils.'

"Homoeroticism and incest also figure as themes. The main female character, Yukiko, draws hair on the 'mound' of a little girl. The brothers of a dead samurai have sex with his daughter. Many things glisten (mouths, hair, evergreens), quiver (a 'pink underlip,' arm muscles, legs), and are sniffed (floorboards, sheets, fingers)."

Considering a few other notable passages, it seems the work might also be useful for parents who are both trying to teach their kids proper grammar and who want to prepare them for that inevitable awkward first sexual experience with dangerous wildlife:

"At age ten the madam put the child in a cage with a bear trained to couple with young girls so the girls would be frigid and not fall in love with their patrons. They fed her through the bars and aroused the bear with a stick when it seemed to lose interest."

Discussion: How could this sentence be improved? Is it the madam who's ten or the child? How would you clear up the ambiguity? Is Lewis Libby a sick fuck or what?

Bill O'Reilly's Those Who Trespass

One of the main characters in Bill O'Reilly's 1998 murder mystery, *Those Who Trespass,* is Shannon Michaels, a television reporter who, coincidentally, sounds a lot like an idealized version of the author:

"His teal blue eyes were locked on the agitated crowd. It was his eyes that most people noticed first—a very unusual color that some thought materialized from a contact lens case. But Shannon, the product of two Celtic parents, didn't go in for cosmetic enhancements. His 6'4" frame was well toned by constant athletics, and his pale white skin was flawless—another genetic gift."

Okay, so change "genetic gift" to "genetic glitch" and this is pretty much a spot-on description of O'Reilly himself.

Why is this important? Flip forward to page 156 and it suddenly becomes clear.

Displaying the deft touch of the old woman who types up the minutes for your town's weekly common council meetings, O'Reilly kicked off his doppelganger's torrid sex romp with fellow reporter Ashley Van Buren thusly:

"Finally, she dictated the course of the evening. 'Okay, Shannon Michaels, off with those pants.'"

The rest of the passage reads more or less like Morley Safer and Richard Speck's failed collaboration on a *Penthouse Forum* letter:

"While still sitting, Shannon undid his belt and the button on his jeans. Very slowly, he lifted his hips, sliding the jeans down his long legs. When they reached his feet, he deftly kicked them off.

"Ashley took it all in. He was wearing Calvin Klein briefs. Black. Her eyes moved downward from his slim hips to his legs. She tried not to stare at his crotch, even though she saw movement there."

He later continued:

"Ashley was now wearing only brief white panties. By removing her shirt and skirt, and by leaning back on the couch, she had signaled her desire. Now, she closed her eyes, concentrating on nothing but Shannon's tongue and lips. He gently teased her by licking the areas around her most sensitive erogenous zone. Then he slipped her panties down her legs and, within seconds, his tongue was inside her, moving rapidly. Ashley felt intense pleasure building. Doubts briefly surfaced, but she quickly dismissed them. She had not felt physical pleasure of this kind for a long time. Maybe it had never been this good. Why should she deny herself? There wasn't any concrete reason why she shouldn't enjoy the moment for a change.

"Ashley climaxed twice before the two got up from the couch and climbed the stairs to the master bedroom. Shannon ignited the logs in the fireplace as Ashley nestled in, under the down comforter. She could see Shannon outlined against the fire, still partially erect."

There's more of course. (The novel's touching conclusion includes the swoon-worthy "Tommy O'Malley was naked and at attention.") But the limits of fair use and common decency urge a quick wrap-up.

Let's just end with this gem, in case you're wondering what sort of clever bons mots traverse Bill's mind 24/7:

"Tommy was already seated at a window table when Ashley walked over and plopped herself down in an overstuffed chair.

"'Whatcha doin', big boy?'

"Tommy turned away from his view of the Atlantic. It was nothing compared to the view of Ashley, he thought."

Somewhere a dog barked, and in the darkening alley, Joseph O'Breuer, an aspiring young book critic, blew his brains out with his mother's polished, pearl-handled revolver. He slumped, lifeless, onto the blood-spattered cobblestones, still partially erect.

PORNO IMPRESARIO PHIL GRAMM

In 1995, Republican Senator Phil Gramm, then a presidential candidate, was embarrassed by allegations that twenty years earlier he'd invested in a soft-core porn movie parody about the Nixon White House.

According to a story in *The New Republic*, Gramm had, through the wife of a colleague, sunk several thousand dollars into a movie called *White House Madness*.

Gramm's former brother-in-law George Caton told the magazine that he'd shown Gramm the rushes of *Truck Stop Women*, another film he'd been working on, and Gramm became as excited as a Bill O'Reilly hero who'd just received a direct, pre-coital instruction to whip his pants off. The film, it seems, was to feature grown-up ladies with their clothes off.

"It really got Phil titillated because there was frontal nudity in it," Caton told *The New Republic*. "He thought it would be a way to make a lot of money."

According to Caton, Gramm initially tried to invest in *Truck Stop Women,* but had to settle for sloppy seconds. Caton returned Gramm's check after telling him the movie already had plenty of investors.

"He was agitated as all get out," recalled Caton. "He made me promise that he would be in the front of the line for the next picture."

The next picture was *Beauty Queens,* a "sexploitation of beauty contests, how all the beauty queens are screwing the contest judges to win," said Caton. "We gave Phil the script to read and he loved it."

But according to Caton, Gramm wanted to remain a silent partner.

"He told me he was contemplating running for political office, and he didn't want the investment in his name. He asked me if I would mind having it in the name of the wife of one of his colleagues."

Eventually, the production team behind *Beauty Queens* decided to scrap the project in favor of *White House Wedding* (later changed to *White House Madness*), an anti-Nixon sex satire.

According to the article, when Caton told Gramm about plans for the new movie "he got even more excited and wanted to put in more money."

The movie ultimately bombed, and Gramm lost his investment.

For his part, Gramm denied the details of Caton's account.

"The statement he has made about my drooling over this . . . film is just totally false. We obviously have an old family vendetta here."

Wrote the *New York Daily News:* "In an earlier statement, Gramm said he innocently thought Caton just 'wanted to get into the movie business' and was flabbergasted to find out that he was helping to produce a bawdy film.

"The senator said 'the ultimate outcome of investing with my brother-in-law was a total loss. He and my wife's sister were divorced in 1975 and that was the last of my $7,500.'"

In its response, *The New Republic* noted that Gramm had changed his story as the scandal unfolded, and that Gramm's explanation was nevertheless implausible: "[Gramm's] reaction to

John B. Judis's article last week . . . is perhaps as worrying as anything in the article itself. It certainly confirms the heart of the story: that Gramm is an opportunist, with few principles, a tendency to dissemble and a shameless desire for power."

Yes, if there's anything more disgusting than a guy who inserts himself into a clumsy sex scene or writes about ten-year-olds fucking bears, it's a man who won't stand by his art.

DIDJAKNOW?

Harvey Pitt, who resigned amid controversy as chairman of the SEC in November 2002, saw his original nomination challenged by antiporn crusaders.

The Traditional Values Coalition, which represents thousands of churches, sent George W. Bush a letter in May of 2001 opposing Pitt's nomination. Their objection stemmed from his work for New Frontier Media, which the group called a "major" pornography distributor.

INDEX